KB007981

1100 Short & Useful Korean Phrases For Beginners

Written by **Talk To Me In Korean**

1100 Short & Useful Korean Phrases For Beginners
패턴으로 배우는 초급 한국어

1판 1쇄 · 1st edition published	2020. 3. 16.
1판 9쇄 · 9th edition published	2024. 6. 24.

지은이 · Written by	Talk To Me In Korean
책임편집 · Edited by	선경화 Kyung-hwa Sun, 대니 드루터 Dani Druther
디자인 · Designed by	선윤아 Yoona Sun, 한보람 Boram Han
삽화 · Illustrations by	장성원 Kanari Jones
녹음 · Voice Recordings by	선현우 Hyunwoo Sun, 최경은 Kyeong-eun Choi
펴낸곳 · Published by	롱테일북스 Longtail Books
펴낸이 · Publisher	이수영 Su Young Lee
편집 · Copy-edited by	김보경 Florence Kim
주소 · Address	04033 서울특별시 마포구 양화로 113, 3층(서교동, 순흥빌딩)
	3rd Floor, 113 Yanghwa-ro, Mapo-gu, Seoul, KOREA
이메일 · E-mail	TTMIK@longtailbooks.co.kr
ISBN	979-11-86701-51-5 13710

*이 교재의 내용을 사전 허가 없이 전재하거나 복제할 경우 법적인 제재를 받게 됨을 알려 드립니다.
*잘못된 책은 구입하신 서점이나 본사에서 교환해 드립니다.
*정가는 표지에 표시되어 있습니다.

Copyright © 2020 Talk To Me In Korean

*All rights reserved. Partial or in full copies of this book are strictly prohibited unless consent or permission is given by the publisher.
*Defective copies of this book may be exchanged at participating bookstores or directly from the publisher.
*The standard price of this book is printed on the back cover above the UPC barcode.

TTMIK - TALK TO ME IN KOREAN

1100 SPEAKING

Short & Useful
Korean Phrases
For Beginners

Let me cast a spell
on your Korean!

Table of Contents

Preface

When you first start learning a new language, everything looks quite complicated and hard to understand. But gradually, words and phrases become more familiar-sounding, and you can start saying simple things more comfortably.

Just like that, you will get used to saying whole phrases and sentences too, but relying on just picking up one sentence here and another sentence there might not be the most efficient way to learn Korean. With this book, you can learn 100 of the most commonly used Korean sentence patterns and practice forming new sentences on your own. This way, instead of only knowing one sentence using a certain structure, you can say things you have never said before and more comfortably, using the sentence patterns introduced in this book.

You can start from the very first pages and go through everything unit by unit, or just pick a sentence structure that you know you will need to use in the near future when speaking or writing in Korean.

Thank you for learning Korean using Talk To Me In Korean's materials, and we hope you enjoy studying with this book as much as we enjoyed creating it!

감사합니다.

TTMIK Team

Quick Guide to Hangeul 한글

The Korean alphabet is called 한글 (Hangeul), and there are 24 basic letters and digraphs in 한글. *digraph: pair of characters used to make one sound (phoneme)

Of the letters, 14 are consonants (자음), and five of them are doubled to form the five tense consonants (쌍자음).

Consonants

Basic

ㄱ	ㄴ	ㄷ	ㄹ	ㅁ	ㅂ	ㅅ
g/k	n	d/t	r/l	m	b/p	s
g/k	n	d/t	r/l	m	b/p	s/ɕ

Tense

ㄲ		ㄸ			ㅃ	ㅆ
kk		tt			pp	ss
k'		t'			p'	s'

The pronunciations of each consonant above, however, apply when the consonant is used as a beginning consonant. When those consonants are used as the final consonant of a syllable block, only seven consonants are pronounced, ㄱ, ㄴ, ㄷ, ㄹ, ㅁ, ㅂ, and ㅇ. The rest of the consonants are pronounced as one of these seven consonants when they are used as a final consonant.

O	ㅈ	ㅊ	ㅋ	ㅌ	ㅍ	ㅎ
ng	j	ch	k	t	p	h
ŋ	dʑ/tɕ	tɕʰ	k/kʰ	t/tʰ	p/pʰ	h

ㅉ
jj
c'

* ㅋ and ㄲ are pronounced as ㄱ when they are used as a final consonant.

* ㅅ, ㅈ, ㅊ, ㅌ, ㅎ, and ㅆ are pronounced as ㄷ when they are used as a final consonant.

* ㅍ is pronounced as ㅂ when used as a final consonant.

* ㄸ, ㅃ, and ㅉ are not used as a final consonant.

When it comes to vowels (모음), there are 10 basic letters. 11 additional letters can be created by combining certain basic letters to make a total of 21 vowels. Of the vowels, eight are single pure vowels, also known as monophthongs (단모음), and 13 are diphthongs (이중모음), or two vowel sounds joined into one syllable which creates one sound.

Vowels

Monophthongs

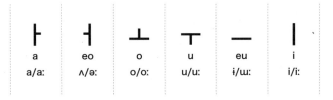

ㅏ	ㅓ	ㅗ	ㅜ	ㅡ	ㅣ
a	eo	o	u	eu	i
a/aː	ʌ/əː	o/oː	u/uː	ɨ/ɯː	i/iː

Diphthongs

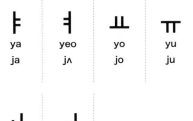

ㅑ	ㅕ	ㅛ	ㅠ
ya	yeo	yo	yu
ja	jʌ	jo	ju

ㅘ	ㅝ
wa	wo
wa	wʌ/wəː

* When saying a monophthong, you are producing one pure vowel with no tongue movement.

* When saying a diphthong, you are producing one sound by saying two vowels. Therefore, your tongue and mouth move quickly from one letter to another (glide or slide) to create a single sound.

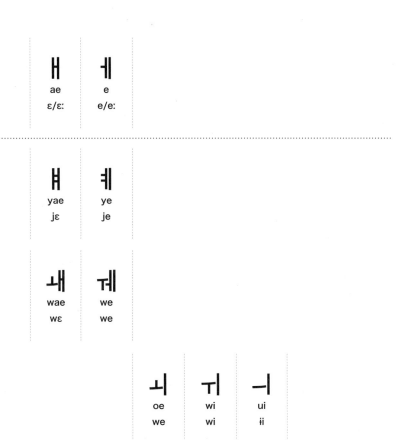

ㅐ	ㅔ
ae	e
ɛ/ɛː	e/eː

ㅒ	ㅖ
yae	ye
jɛ	je

ㅙ	ㅞ
wae	we
wɛ	we

ㅚ	ㅟ	ㅢ
oe	wi	ui
we	wi	ïi

* ㅚ and ㅟ were pronounced as single pure vowels (monophthongs) in the past; however, presently, these vowels are produced as two vowels gradually gliding into one another to create one sound (diphthong).

Writing 한글 Letters

한글 is written top to bottom, left to right. For example:

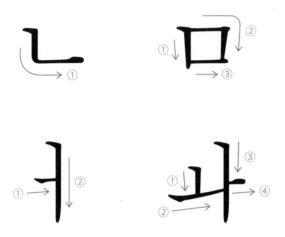

By making sure you follow the stroke order rules, you will find that writing Korean is quite easy, and other people will be able to better read your handwriting.

Syllable Blocks

Each Korean syllable is written in a way that forms a block-like shape, with each letter inside the block forming a sound/syllable.

In each syllable block, there is a:

1. * Beginning consonant

2. * Middle vowel

3. Optional final consonant

* Required in a syllable block. A block MUST contain a minimum of two letters: one consonant and one vowel.

ㅊ + ㅣ + ㄴ (ch + i + n) = chin

ㄱ + ㅜ (g + u) = gu

친 (chin) + 구 (gu) = 친구 (chingu) = "friend"

Two of the most common ways to write consonant and vowel combinations in Korean are horizontally and vertically (the boxes drawn here are for illustrative purpose only).

By adding a final consonant (받침), the blocks are modified:

There are also syllables which have two final consonants, such as:

* In all the syllable blocks, the letters are either compressed or
stretched to keep the size relatively the same as the other letters.

Place Holder In Front Of Vowels

Since the "minimum two letter" rule exists, and one letter has to be a consonant and the other has to be a vowel, what can you do when a vowel needs to be written in its own syllable block? Add the consonant ㅇ [ng] in front of or on top of the vowel. When reading a vowel, such as 아, the ㅇ makes no sound, and you just pronounce the ㅏ [a].

* Vowels absolutely cannot—under any circumstances—be written by themselves!!

Okay!
Now that you are equipped with a basic knowledge
of 한글, it is time to do your part and start
practicing! Let's get to it!

How to Use This Book

You are introduced to a new sentence structure "pattern" here. Practice making sentences just by filling in the blank with any word.

If there is something you should know when filling in the blank, it will be written here.

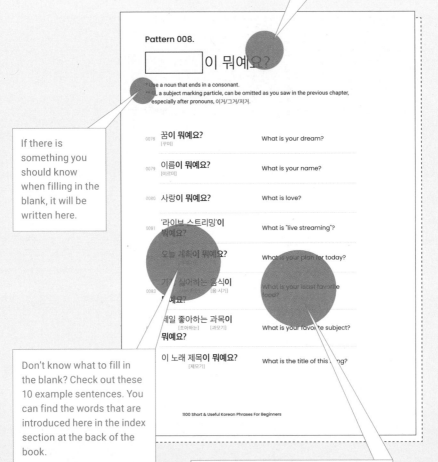

Pattern 008.

☐ 이 뭐예요?

* Use a noun that ends in a consonant.
** 이, a subject marking particle, can be omitted as you saw in the previous chapter, especially after pronouns, 이거/그거/저거.

0078	꿈이 뭐예요? [꾸미]	What is your dream?
0079	이름이 뭐예요? [이르미]	What is your name?
0080	사랑이 뭐예요?	What is love?
0081	'라이브 스트리밍'이 뭐예요?	What is "live streaming"?
	오늘 계획이 뭐예요?	What is your plan for today?
0083	가장 싫어하는 음식이 뭐예요? [음·시기]	What is your least favorite food?
	제일 좋아하는 과목이 [조아하는] [과모기] 뭐예요?	What is your favorite subject?
	이 노래 제목이 뭐예요? [제모기]	What is the title of this song?

1100 Short & Useful Korean Phrases For Beginners

Don't know what to fill in the blank? Check out these 10 example sentences. You can find the words that are introduced here in the index section at the back of the book.

Korean sentences are on the left, and their English meanings are on the right on the page. After you learn all the sentences, cover the left side and try to say in Korean just by looking at the English meanings.

The English meaning of the "pattern" for each unit is written at the top-right of the page. The "N" stands for "noun". The "V" stands for "verb". The "Adj" stands for "adjective", and the "S" stands for "subject".

If you scan the QR code here, the audio will automatically play, and you can listen to native speakers' pronunciation. If you cannot use QR codes, you can also listen to the audio and download it on our website, **https://talktomeinkorean.com/audio**.

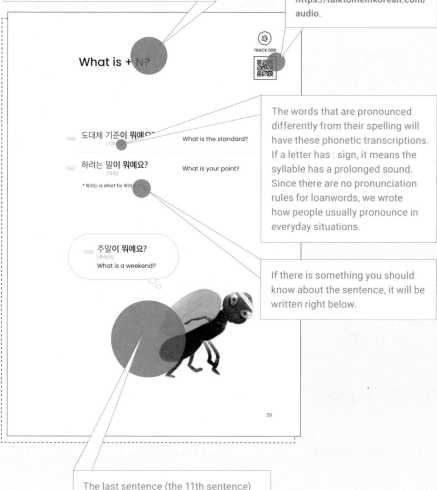

What is + N?

TRACK 008

0086 도대체 기준이 뭐예요?
[기준]
What is the standard?

0087 하려는 말이 뭐예요?
[마리]
What is your point?
* 하려는 is short for 하려고

The words that are pronounced differently from their spelling will have these phonetic transcriptions. If a letter has : sign, it means the syllable has a prolonged sound. Since there are no pronunciation rules for loanwords, we wrote how people usually pronounce in everyday situations.

0088 주말이 뭐예요?
[주마리]
What is a weekend?

If there is something you should know about the sentence, it will be written right below.

39

The last sentence (the 11th sentence) for each unit is a bonus. Since it is introduced with a funny drawing, it will be easy to remember.

Pattern 001.

예요.

* You add -예요 to the nouns that end with a vowel.

0001 친구**예요**.   This is my friend.

0002 강아지**예요**.   This is a dog.

0003 저**예요**.   It is me.

0004 이거**예요**.   It is this. (This is what I meant.)

0005 커피**예요**.   This is coffee.

0006 이 차**예요**.   It is this tea.
(This tea is what I meant.)

0007 친한 친구**예요**.   This is my close friend.

0008 뜨거운 커피**예요**.   This is hot coffee.

This is + N. / It is + N.

0009 고장 난 시계**예요.**　　　　　It is a broken clock.

0010 제 동생 컴퓨터**예요.**　　　　　It is my younger sister/brother's computer.

* In casual spoken language, the possessive particle, -의, is often dropped. 제 동생의 컴퓨터예요 sounds more formal and written.

0011 바보**예요.**
They are a fool.

Pattern 002.

이에요.

* Use the nouns that end in a consonant.

0012 **책이에요.**
[채기에요]

This is a book.

0013 **선물이에요.**
[선:무리에요]

This is a present.

0014 **물이에요.**
[무리에요]

This is water.

0015 **오늘이에요.**
[오느리에요]

It is today.

0016 제 사진**이에요.**
[사지니에요]

This is a picture of me.

0017 제 가방**이에요.**

This is my bag.

0018 차가운 물**이에요.**
[무리에요]

This is cold water.

0019 좋은 사람**이에요.**
[조은]　[사:라미에요]

He/she is a good person.

This is + N. / It is + N.

0020 **좀 비싼 옷이에요.**
[오시에요]

These are somewhat expensive clothes.

0021 **제가 좋아하는 사람이에요.**
[조아하는]　[사:라미에요]

This is a person that I like.

0022 **제 경호원이에요.**
[경호워니에요]
This is my bodyguard.

Pattern 003.

[   ] 아니에요.

0023 이거 **아니에요**.   It is not this one.

0024 저 **아니에요**.   It is not me.

0025 친구 **아니에요**.   He/she is not my friend.

0026 선물 **아니에요**.   This is not a present.

0027 쓰레기 **아니에요**.   This is not trash.

0028 나쁜 사람 **아니에요**.   He/she is not a bad person.

0029 제 가방 **아니에요**.   This is not my bag.

0030 이 버스 **아니에요**.
[버쓰/뻐쓰]   It is not this bus.

This is not + N. / It is not + N.

0031 제 생일 **아니에요.**　　　　It is not my birthday.

0032 제가 산 물건 **아니에요.**　　This is not what I bought.

0033 배신자 **아니에요.**
I am not a betrayer.

Pattern 004.

 있어요.

* 있다 can mean "to have" or "to exist," so 있어요 can mean "I have..." or "There is...".

0034 **시간 있어요.**
[이써요]

I have time.

0035 **돈 있어요.**
[이써요]

I have money.

0036 **펜 있어요.**
[이써요]

I have a pen.

0037 **질문 있어요.**
[이써요]

I have a question.

0038 **고민 있어요.**
[이써요]

I have a concern.

0039 **좋은 생각 있어요.**
[조은]   [이써요]

I have a good idea.

0040 **따뜻한 차 있어요.**
[따뜨탄]   [이써요]

There is warm tea.

0041 **질문이 하나 있어요.**
[질무니]   [이써요]

I have one question.

I have + N. / There is + N.

0042 **저기에 있어요.**
[이써요]

It is over there.

0043 **제 자전거는 1층에 있어요.**
[일층에] [이써요]

My bicycle is on the first floor.

0044 **귀신 있어요.**
[이써요]
There is a ghost.

Pattern 005.

[   ] 없어요.

0045	시간 **없어요.** [업써요]	I do not have time.
0046	돈 **없어요.** [업써요]	I do not have money.
0047	문제 **없어요.** [업써요]	There is no problem.
0048	약속 **없어요.** [약쏙] [업써요]	I do not have any plans.
0049	명함 **없어요.** [업써요]	I do not have business cards.
0050	외국인 친구 **없어요.** [외:구긴] [업써요]	I do not have international friends.
0051	그런 거 **없어요.** [업써요]	There is no such thing.
0052	하고 싶은 거 **없어요.** [시픈] [업써요]	I do not have anything I want to do.

I do not have + N. /
There is not + N.

0053 먹고 싶은 거 **없어요.**
[먹꼬] [시픈] [업써요]

I do not have anything I want to eat.

0054 여기에 아무도 **없어요.**
[업써요]

There is no one here.

0055 관심 **없어요.**
[업써요]
I do not have an interest in it. /
I am not interested.

Pattern 006.

┌─────────┐ 주세요.
└─────────┘

0056	이거 **주세요.**	Please give this to me.
0057	용돈 **주세요.** [용:똔]	Please give me some allowance.
0058	커피 **주세요.**	Please give me coffee.
0059	힌트 **주세요.**	Please give me some hints.
0060	연락처 **주세요.** [열락처]	Please give me your contact information.
0061	따뜻한 물 **주세요.** [따뜨탄]	Please give me warm water.
0062	컵 하나 **주세요.**	Please give me a cup.

* Unless you pause between 컵 and 하나, 컵 하나 is pronounced as [커 파나].

0063	초콜릿 빵 **주세요.** [초콜릳]	Please give me some chocolate bread.

Please give me + N.

0064   빨대 세 개 **주세요.**
　　　[빨때]

Please give me three straws.

0065   장미 꽃 세 송이 **주세요.**
　　　　　[꼳]

Please give me three roses.

0066   **지갑 주세요.**
　　　Please give me your wallet.

Pattern 007.

☐☐☐☐ 뭐예요?

0067 이거 **뭐예요?**　　　　　　　What is this?

0068 그거 **뭐예요?**　　　　　　　What is it?

0069 저기 저거 **뭐예요?**　　　　　What is that over there?

0070 비밀번호 **뭐예요?**　　　　　What is the password?

0071 웹사이트 주소 **뭐예요?**
[웹싸이트]　　　　　　　　　　What is the website address?

0072 책 제목 **뭐예요?**　　　　　　What is the book title?

0073 노래 제목 **뭐예요?**　　　　　What is the song title?

0074 그 티셔츠 **뭐예요?**　　　　　What is that T-shirt?

What is + N?

0075 손에 있는 그거 **뭐예요?**
[소네] [인는]

What is that in your hand?

0076 테이블 위에 있는 저거
[인는]
뭐예요?

What is that on the table?

0077 신용 카드 비밀번호 **뭐예요?**
[시:농]
What is your credit card PIN?

Pattern 008.

이 뭐예요?

* Use a noun that ends in a consonant.

** 이, a subject marking particle, can be omitted as you saw in the previous chapter, especially after pronouns, 이거/그거/저거.

0078	**꿈이 뭐예요?** [꾸미]	What is your dream?
0079	**이름이 뭐예요?** [이르미]	What is your name?
0080	**사랑이 뭐예요?**	What is love?
0081	**'라이브 스트리밍'이 뭐예요?**	What is "live streaming"?
0082	**오늘 계획이 뭐예요?** [계:회기]	What is your plan for today?
0083	**가장 싫어하는 음식이** [시러하는]　[음·시기] **뭐예요?**	What is your least favorite food?
0084	**제일 좋아하는 과목이** [조아하는]　[과모기] **뭐예요?**	What is your favorite subject?
0085	**이 노래 제목이 뭐예요?** [제모기]	What is the title of this song?

What is + N?

0086 **도대체 기준이 뭐예요?**
[기주니]

What is the standard?

0087 **하려는 말이 뭐예요?**
[마리]

What is your point?

* 하려는 is short for 하려고 하는.

0088 **주말이 뭐예요?**
[주마리]
What is a weekend?

Pattern 009.

가 뭐예요?

* Use a noun that ends in a vowel.

0089	취미**가 뭐예요?**	What is your hobby?
0090	문제**가 뭐예요?**	What is the problem?
0091	'미세 먼지'**가 뭐예요?**	What is "microdust"?
0092	'장마'**가 뭐예요?**	What is a "monsoon"?
0093	장르**가 뭐예요?**	What is its genre?
0094	이유**가 뭐예요?**	What is the reason?
0095	그 소설은 장르**가 뭐예요?** [소:설른]	What is the genre of the novel?
0096	좋아하는 스포츠**가 뭐예요?** [조아하는]	Which sports do you like?

What is + N?

0097 제일 좋아하는 영화**가**
[조아하는]
뭐예요?

What is your favorite movie?

0098 그렇게 생각하는 이유**가**
[그러케] [생가카는]
뭐예요?

What is the reason that you think so?

0099 '아아'**가 뭐예요?**
What is 아아?

Pattern 010.

혹시  예요/이에요?

* Attach -예요 to a noun that ends in a vowel. Otherwise, attach -이에요.

0100	**혹시** 이거**예요?** [혹씨]	By any chance, is this what you said?
0101	**혹시** 여기**예요?** [혹씨]	By any chance, is this where you meant?
0102	**혹시** 학생**이에요?** [혹씨] [학쌩이에요]	By any chance, are you a student?
0103	**혹시** 외계인**이에요?** [혹씨] [외:계이니에요]	By any chance, are you an alien?
0104	**혹시** 아는 사람**이에요?** [혹씨] [사:라미에요]	By any chance, is it someone you know?
0105	**혹시** 호주 사람**이에요?** [혹씨] [사:라미에요]	By any chance, are you an Australian?
0106	**혹시** 이거 정답**이에요?** [혹씨] [정:다비에요]	By any chance, is this the right answer?
0107	**혹시** 지금 시험 기간**이에요?** [혹씨] [기가니에요]	By any chance, is it exam period now?

By any chance, is it + N? /
By any chance, are you + N?

0108 저 사람 **혹시** 연예인**이에요?**
[혹씨] [여:녜이니에요]

By any chance, is that person a celebrity?

0109 저 사람 **혹시** 석진 씨
[혹씨] [석찐]
동생**이에요?**

By any chance, is that person Seokjin's younger brother/ sister?

0110 **혹시** 바보**예요?**
[혹씨]

By any chance, are you a fool?

43

Pattern 011.

□□□□ 에 가요.

0111	**학교에 가요.** [학꾜에]	I go to school.
0112	**회사에 가요.**	I go to the office.
0113	**카페에 가요.** [까페에]	I go to a cafe.
0114	**백화점에 가요.** [배콰저메]	I go to a department store.
0115	**일찍 집에 가요.** [지베]	I go home early.
0116	**아침에 산에 가요.** [아치메]　[사네]	I go to the mountain in the morning.
0117	**금요일에 강남에 가요.** [그묘이레]　[강나메]	I go to Gangnam on Friday.
0118	**주말에 교회에 가요.** [주마레]	I go to church on weekends.

I go to + N. /
I am going to + N.

0119 **친구랑 학원에 가요.**
[하궈네]

I go to cram school with my friend.

0120 **아빠랑 병원에 가요.**
[병워네]

I go to the hospital with my dad.

0121 **친구랑 경찰서에 가요.**
[경찰써에]
I go to the police station with my friend.

Pattern 012.

 에 있어요.

0122	**집에 있어요.** [지베]　[이써요]	It is at home.
0123	**편의점에 있어요.** [펴니저메]　　[이써요]	It is at a convenience store.
0124	**가방에 있어요.** 　　　[이써요]	It is in the bag.
0125	**저기에 있어요.** 　　　[이써요]	It is over there.
0126	**6층에 있어요.** [육층에]　[이써요]	It is on the sixth floor.
0127	**한국에 있어요.** [한:구게]　[이써요]	It is in Korea.
0128	**전부 여기에 있어요.** 　　　　[이써요]	All of them are here.
0129	**제 옆에 있어요.** 　[여페]　[이써요]	It is next to me.

It is in/at + N. /
I am in/at + N.

0130 **경화 씨 옆에 있어요.**
[여페] [이써요]

It is next to Kyung-hwa.

0131 **백화점 근처에 있어요.**
[배콰점] [이써요]

It is near the department store.

0132 **공룡은 저희 집에 있어요.**
[공ː뇽은] [저히] [지베] [이써요]
The dinosaur is in my house.

Pattern 013.

[   ] 어디에 있어요?

0133   화장실 **어디에 있어요?**
[이써요]

Where is the restroom?

0134   물티슈 **어디에 있어요?**
[이써요]

Where are wet wipes?

0135   수저 **어디에 있어요?**
[이써요]

Where are spoons and chopsticks?

0136   서류 **어디에 있어요?**
[이써요]

Where is the document?

0137   그거 **어디에 있어요?**
[이써요]

Where is it?

0138   가위 **어디에 있어요?**
[이써요]

Where are scissors?

0139   주연 씨 **어디에 있어요?**
[이써요]

Where is Jooyeon?

0140   석진 씨 지갑 **어디에 있어요?**
[석찐]   [이써요]

Where is Seokjin's wallet?

Where is + N?

0141
그때 말한 가게 **어디에 있어요?**
[이써요]

Where is the store that we talked about the other day?

0142
제일 가까운 주유소는 **어디에 있어요?**
[이써요]

Where is the nearest gas station?

0143 제 페라리 **어디에 있어요?**
[이써요]

Where is my Ferrari?

Pattern 014.

☐☐☐☐☐에 가는 길이에요.

0144 집에 가는 길이에요.
[지베] [기리에요]
I am on my way home.

0145 부산에 가는 길이에요.
[부사네] [기리에요]
I am on my way to Busan.

0146 회사에 가는 길이에요.
[기리에요]
I am on my way to the office.

0147 은행에 가는 길이에요.
[기리에요]
I am on my way to a bank.

0148 친구 집에 가는 길이에요.
[지베] [기리에요]
I am on my way to my friend's place.

0149 백화점에 가는 길이에요.
[배콰저메] [기리에요]
I am on my way to a department store.

0150 좋아하는 카페에 가는
[조아하는] [까페에]
길이에요.
[기리에요]
I am on my way to a cafe that I like.

0151 아빠랑 수영장에 가는
길이에요.
[기리에요]
I am on my way to a pool with my dad.

I am on my way to + N.

0152
동생이랑 공항**에 가는
길이에요**.
[기리에요]

I am on my way to an airport
with my younger brother/sister.

0153
서울에 있는 미술관**에 가는**
[서우레]　　[인는]　[미술과네]
길이에요.
[기리에요]

I am on my way to an art
gallery in Seoul.

0154 지하 50층**에 가는 길이에요**.
　　　　[오십층에]　　　　[기리에요]
I am on my way to the 50th
basement floor.

Pattern 015.

이/가 언제예요?

* Attach -가 to a noun that ends in a vowel. Otherwise, attach -이.

0155 **생일이 언제예요?**
[생이리]

When is your birthday?

0156 **월급날이 언제예요?**
[월금나리]

When is your pay day?

0157 **휴가가 언제예요?**

When is your day off?

0158 **방학이 언제예요?**
[방하기]

When is your vacation?

0159 **결혼기념일이 언제예요?**
[결혼기녀미리]

When is your wedding anniversary?

0160 **중간고사가 언제예요?**

When are your midterms?

0161 **기말고사가 언제예요?**

When is your final exam?

0162 **세일 기간이 언제예요?**
[쎄일] [기가니]

When is the sale period?

When is + N?

0163 **입학식이 언제예요?**
[이팍씨기]

When is your school entrance ceremony?

0164 **졸업식이 언제예요?**
[조럽씨기]

When is your graduation ceremony?

0165 **제 결혼식이 언제예요?**
[결혼시기]
When is my wedding?

Pattern 016.

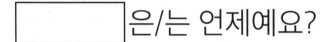 은/는 언제예요?

* Attach -은 to a noun that ends in a consonant. Otherwise, attach -는.

0166 **축제는 언제예요?**
[축쩨는]

As for the festival, when is it?

0167 **회식은 언제예요?**
[회시근]

As for the company dinner, when is it?

0168 **봄 방학은 언제예요?**
[방하근]

As for spring break, when is it?

* People often pronounce 봄 방학 as [봄 빵학] when they do not pause between 봄 and 방학.

0169 **그 행사는 언제예요?**

As for the event, when is it?

0170 **제 차례는 언제예요?**

As for my turn, when is it?

0171 **다음 회의는 언제예요?**

As for the next meeting, when is it?

0172 **이번 달 모임은 언제예요?**
[이번 딸]   [모이믄]

As for this month's gathering, when is it?

0173 **미술 수업은 언제예요?**
[수어븐]

As for the art class, when is it?

As for + N, when is it?

0174 그 사람 생일은 언제예요?
[생이른]

As for his/her birthday, when is it?

0175 동생 결혼식은 언제예요?
[결혼시근]

As for your younger brother/ sister's wedding ceremony, when is it?

0176 제 생일은 언제예요?
[생이른]

As for my birthday, when is it?

Pattern 017.

벌써 [   ] 예요/이에요?

0177	**벌써** 10시**예요?** [열씨예요]	Is it already 10 o'clock?
0178	**벌써** 끝**이에요?** [끄치에요]	Is it already over?
0179	**벌써** 졸업**이에요?** [조러비에요]	Is it already your graduation?
0180	**벌써** 다섯 살**이에요?** [다섣 싸리에요]	Is he/she already five?
0181	**벌써** 초등학생**이에요?** [초등학쌩이에요]	Does he/she go to elementary school already?
0182	**벌써** 마감**이에요?** [마가미에요]	Are you already closing up?
0183	**벌써** 아침**이에요?** [아치미에요]	Is it already morning?
0184	**벌써** 금요일**이에요?** [그묘이리에요]	Is it already Friday?

Is it already + N?

0185 **벌써 퇴근 시간이에요?**
[시가니에요]

Is it already time to get off work?

0186 **벌써 결혼 3주년이에요?**
[삼주녀니에요]

Is it already your third wedding anniversary?

0187 **벌써 1,000살이에요?**
[천사리에요]

Is he already 1,000 years old?

Pattern 018.

⬜⬜⬜ 이/가 좋아요.

0188	이 카페**가 좋아요.** [까페] [조아요]	I like this cafe.
0189	편한 바지**가 좋아요.** [조아요]	I like comfortable pants.
0190	저는 여기**가 좋아요.** [조아요]	I like this place.
0191	저는 이 노래**가 좋아요.** [조아요]	I like this song.
0192	저는 바나나 주스**가 좋아요.** [주쓰가] [조아요]	I like banana juice.
0193	저는 이 노래**가** 제일 **좋아요.** [조아요]	I like this song the most.
0194	저는 이 아이디어**가** 제일 **좋아요.** [조아요]	I like this idea the most.
0195	저는 이탈리아**가** 제일 **좋아요.** [조아요]	I like Italy the most.

I like + N.

0196 **저는 여름이 제일 좋아요.**
[여르미] [조아요]

I like summer the most.

0197 **저는 국내 여행이 더 좋아요.**
[궁내] [조아요]

I like domestic travel more.

0198 **저는 잘생긴 남자가 좋아요.**
[조아요]

I like handsome guys.

Pattern 019.

그리고 [ ]도 있어요.

0199	그리고 저도 있어요. [이써요]	And there is also me.
0200	그리고 상금도 있어요. [이써요]	And there is also prize money.
0201	그리고 상품도 있어요. [이써요]	And there are also prizes.
0202	그리고 재미도 있어요. [이써요]	And it is also fun.
0203	그리고 사슴도 있어요. [이써요]	And there are also some deer.
0204	그리고 이런 것도 있어요. [걷또] [이써요]	And there is also something like this.
0205	그리고 어린아이도 있어요. [어리나이도] [이써요]	And there is also a child.
0206	그리고 조용한 노래도 있어요. [이써요]	And there are also quiet songs.

* Since people do not necessarily use the plural marker, -들, in Korean, you need to understand whether the noun is singular or plural based on the context.

And there is/are also + N.

0207 **그리고** 안 가는 사람**도 있어요.**
[이써요]

And there is also a person that is not going.

0208 **그리고** 채소 싫어하는
[시러하는]
사람**도 있어요.**
[이써요]

And there is also a person that hates vegetables.

0209 **그리고** 무서운 괴물**도 있어요.**
[이써요]

And there is also a scary monster.

Pattern 020.

☐☐☐☐☐☐ 좋아해요.

0210 운동 **좋아해요.**
[조아해요]

I like exercise.

0211 영화 **좋아해요.**
[조아해요]

I like movies.

0212 아이스크림 **좋아해요.**
[조아해요]

I like ice cream.

0213 커피 **좋아해요.**
[조아해요]

I like coffee.

0214 커피 엄청 **좋아해요.**
[조아해요]

I like coffee a lot.

0215 초콜릿 정말 **좋아해요.**
[초콜릳]   [조아해요]

I like chocolate a lot.

0216 늦잠 자는 거 **좋아해요.**
[늗짬]   [조아해요]

I like getting up late.

* You can turn a verb into a noun by adding -는 거 to the verb stem.

0217 책 읽는 거 **좋아해요.**
[잉는]   [조아해요]

I like reading books.

I like + N.

0218 저도 라면 먹는 거 **좋아해요.**
　　　　　[멍는]　　　[조아해요]

I like eating ramyeon too.

0219 저도 동물원 가는 거 정말
　　　　[동·무뤈]
좋아해요.
[조아해요]

I really like going to the zoo too.

0220 비싼 선물 **좋아해요.**
　　　　　　　[조아해요]
I like expensive gifts.

Pattern 021.

 좋아하세요?

* "좋아하세요?" is a politer version of "좋아해요?"

0221 **여행 좋아하세요?**
[조아하세요]

Do you like travel?

0222 **저 좋아하세요?**
[조아하세요]

Do you like me?

0223 **한국 음식 좋아하세요?**
[조아하세요]

Do you like Korean food?

0224 **이런 음악 좋아하세요?**
[으막] [조아하세요]

Do you like this kind of music?

0225 **비 오는 날 좋아하세요?**
[조아하세요]

Do you like rainy days?

0226 **복숭아 향 좋아하세요?**
[복쑹아] [조아하세요]

Do you like peach scent?

0227 **어떤 커피 좋아하세요?**
[조아하세요]

What kind of coffee do you like?

0228 **어떤 책 좋아하세요?**
[조아하세요]

What kind of books do you like?

Do you like + N?

0229 사진 찍는 거 **좋아하세요?**
　　　[찍는]　　　[조아하세요]

Do you like taking photos?

0230 산책하는 거 **좋아하세요?**
　　　[산채카는]　　　[조아하세요]

Do you like taking a walk?

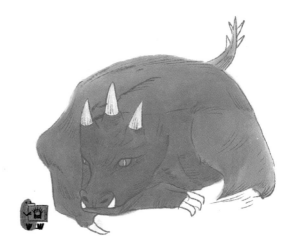

0231 '왕좌의 게임' **좋아하세요?**
　　　　　　[께임]　　[조아하세요]

Do you like *Game Of Thrones*?

Pattern 022.

☐ 어때요?

0232	이거 **어때요?**	How about this?
0233	커피 **어때요?**	How about coffee?
0234	내일 **어때요?**	How about tomorrow?
0235	이 옷 **어때요?**	How about these clothes?
0236	이런 장갑 **어때요?**	How about this kind of glove?
0237	저기 **어때요?**	How about there?
0238	박물관 **어때요?** [방물관]	How about a museum?
0239	선물로 장미꽃 **어때요?** [장미꼳]	How about roses for a gift?

How about + N? /
How about + V-ing?

0240 직접 만드는 거 **어때요?**
[직쩝]

How about making it yourself?

0241 한번 가 보는 거 **어때요?**

How about going there?

0242 김치 커피 **어때요?**
How about some kimchi coffee?

Pattern 023.

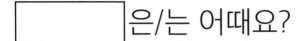

은/는 어때요?

* 은/는 here implies that the noun you are suggesting is just one of many options.

0243 **보라색은 어때요?**
[보라새근]
How about purple?

0244 **여기는 어때요?**
How about this place?

0245 **저기는 어때요?**
How about that place?

0246 **고구마는 어때요?**
How about sweet potatoes?

0247 **이런 디자인은 어때요?**
[디자이는]
How about this kind of design?

0248 **분홍색 바지는 어때요?**
How about pink pants?

0249 **해외 여행은 어때요?**
How about traveling abroad?

0250 **민트 맛 아이스크림은**
[맏] [아이스크리믄]
어때요?
How about mint-flavored ice cream?

How/What about + N?

0251	**저녁으로 삼겹살은 어때요?** [저녀그로]　　[삼겹싸른]	How about grilled pork belly for dinner?
0252	**생일 선물로 돈은 어때요?** 　　　　　[도:는]	How about money for a birthday present?

0253 **생일 선물로 나비는 어때요?**
How about a butterfly for a birthday present?

Pattern 024.

☐☐☐☐☐☐ 어떤 것 같아요?

0254 **이거 어떤 것 같아요?**
[걷] [가타요]

What do you think about this?

0255 **여기 어떤 것 같아요?**
[걷] [가타요]

What do you think about this place?

0256 **가격 어떤 것 같아요?**
[걷] [가타요]

What do you think about the price?

0257 **날씨 어떤 것 같아요?**
[걷] [가타요]

What do you think about the weather?

0258 **이 집 어떤 것 같아요?**
[걷] [가타요]

What do you think about this house?

0259 **저 코트 어떤 것 같아요?**
[걷] [가타요]

What do you think about that coat?

0260 **이 아이디어 어떤 것 같아요?**
[걷] [가타요]

What do you think about this idea?

0261 **제 머리 색깔 어떤 것 같아요?**
[걷] [가타요]

What do you think about my hair color?

What do you think about/of + N?

0262 이거 선물로
어떤 것 같아요?
[걷] [가타요]

What do you think of this as a gift?

0263 여기 혼자 살기에
어떤 것 같아요?
[걷] [가타요]

What do you think of this place for living alone?

0264 저 **어떤 것 같아요?**
[걷] [가타요]
What do you think about me?

Pattern 025.

그러면 [   ] 은/는 어때요?

0265 **그러면 저는 어때요?**

Then, how about me?

0266 **그러면 이거는 어때요?**

Then, how about this one?

0267 **그러면 노래방은 어때요?**

Then, how about the singing room?

0268 **그러면 비빔밥은 어때요?**
[비빔빠븐]

Then, how about bibimbap?

0269 **그러면 놀이공원은 어때요?**
[노리공워는]

Then, how about the amusement park?

0270 **그러면 인터넷 쇼핑은**
[인터넫]
어때요?

Then, how about online shopping?

0271 **그러면 패키지 여행은**
어때요?

Then, how about a package tour?

0272 **그러면 일요일은 어때요?**
[이료이른]

Then, what about Sunday?

Then, how/what about + N?

0273 **그러면 다음 주는 어때요?**
[다음 쭈는]

Then, what about next week?

0274 **그러면 제주도는 어때요?**

Then, how about Jeju Island?

0275 **그러면 50년 뒤는 어때요?**
[오심년]

Then, how about 50 years later?

Pattern 026.

☐ 은/는 별로예요.

0276 여기는 **별로예요.**　　This place is not so good.

0277 맛은 **별로예요.**
[마슨]　　It does not taste that great.

0278 분위기는 **별로예요.**
[부뉘기는]　　Its mood is not that great.

0279 그 방법은 **별로예요.**
[방버븐]　　That way is not that great.

0280 그 생각은 **별로예요.**
[생가근]　　That idea is not so good.

0281 빨간색 양말은 **별로예요.**
[양마른]　　Red socks are not that great (to me).

0282 하와이안 피자는 **별로예요.**　　Hawaiian pizza does not taste so good.

0283 제이슨 씨 의견은 **별로예요.**
[제이쓴]　　[의:겨는]　　Jason's idea is not that great.

N + is not so good. /
N + is not that great.

0284 서비스랑 양은 **별로예요.**
[써비쓰랑]

Their service and portions are not so good.

0285 솔직히 거기는 **별로예요.**
[솔찌키]

To be honest, that place is not so good.

0286 솔직히 그 사람 성격은 **별로예요.**
[솔찌키]   [성:껴근]

To be honest, his personality is not so good.

Pattern 027.

[   ] 은/는 안 돼요?

0287	이거는 **안 돼요?**	Is this not possible?
0288	예약은 **안 돼요?** [예:야근]	Do you not take reservations?
0289	포장은 **안 돼요?**	Is to-go not available?
0290	할인은 **안 돼요?** [하리는]	Is a discount not possible?
0291	다음 주는 **안 돼요?** [다음 쭈는]	Is it not available next week?
0292	슬리퍼는 **안 돼요?**	Are slippers not okay?
0293	지금 확인은 **안 돼요?** [화기는]	Is it not possible to check now?
0294	집까지 배달은 **안 돼요?** [배:다른]	Do you not do home delivery?

Is + N + not available/possible?

0295 1층에서 식사는 안 돼요?
[일층에서]　[식싸는]

Is dining not available on the first floor?

0296 그 사람이랑 직접 통화는
[사:라미랑]　　[직쩝]
안 돼요?

Is it not possible to talk to the person directly on the phone?

0297 일등석은 안 돼요?
[일뜽서근]

Is first class not available?

Pattern 028.

먼저 [   ]부터 해야 돼요.

0298 먼저 이것**부터 해야 돼요.**
[이걷뿌터]
I should do this first.

0299 먼저 숙제**부터 해야 돼요.**
[숙쩨부터]
I should do homework first.

0300 먼저 준비 운동**부터 해야 돼요.**
I should do warm-up exercise first.

0301 먼저 방 청소**부터 해야 돼요.**
I should clean my room first.

0302 먼저 자기소개**부터 해야 돼요.**
You should introduce yourself first.

0303 먼저 회원 가입**부터 해야 돼요.**
[가입뿌터]
You should sign up first.

0304 먼저 제 것**부터 해야 돼요.**
[걷뿌터]
I should do mine first.

0305 먼저 급한 것**부터 해야 돼요.**
[그판] [걷뿌터]
You should do what is urgent first.

I should do + N + first. / You should do + N + first.

0306 **먼저 중요한 일부터 해야 돼요.**

You should do what is important first.

0307 **먼저 하기 싫은 일부터 해야**
[시른]
돼요.

You should do what you do not want to do first.

0308 **먼저 경찰에 신고부터 해야 돼요.**
[경차레]
You should report to the police first.

Pattern 029.

 밖에 없어요.

0309

이거밖에 없어요.
[이거바께]　　[업써요]

This is the only one that I have.

0310

조금밖에 없어요.
[조금바께]　　[업써요]

There is only a little.

0311

과자밖에 없어요.
[과자바께]　　[업써요]

There is nothing but snacks.

0312

이 방법밖에 없어요.
　　[방법빠께]　　[업써요]

This is the only way we have.

0313

빨간색 모자밖에 없어요.
　　　[모자바께]　　[업써요]

There are only red hats.

0314

저는 운동화밖에 없어요.
　　[운동화바께]　　[업써요]

I only have sneakers.

0315

집에 아빠밖에 없어요.
[지베]　[아빠바께]　　[업써요]

It is only my dad who is in the house.

0316

이 사진은 한 장밖에 없어요.
　[사지는]　　　[장바께]　[업써요]

There is only one copy of this photo.

There is only + N. / There is nothing but + N.

0317

지금 사무실에 저**밖에**
[사무시레]　　[저바께]

없어요.
[업써요]

It is only me in the office now.

0318

이 동네에는 식당**밖에**
[식땅바께]

없어요.
[업써요]

There is nothing but restaurants in this town.

0319 저는 자랑할 게 얼굴**밖에 없어요.**
[자랑할 께]　　　[얼굴바께]　　[업써요]
I only have my face to boast about.

Pattern 030.

`[          ]` 이/가 무슨 뜻이에요?

0320	**'명함'이 무슨 뜻이에요?** [명하미]　　　　[뜨시에요]	What does "myeong-ham" mean?
0321	**'이야기'가 무슨 뜻이에요?** 　　　　　　[뜨시에요]	What does "i-ya-gi" mean?
0322	**'인스타'가 무슨 뜻이에요?** 　　　　　[뜨시에요]	What does "in-seu-ta" mean?
0323	**TTMIK가 무슨 뜻이에요?** 　　　　　[뜨시에요]	What does TTMIK mean?
0324	**'웹툰'이 무슨 뜻이에요?** [웹투니]　　　　[뜨시에요]	What does "wep-tun" mean?
0325	**'발이 넓다'가 무슨 뜻이에요?** [바리]　[널따가]　　　　[뜨시에요]	What does "to have wide feet" mean?

* This is an idiomatic phrase that actually means "to have a wide network."

0326	**'눈이 높다'가 무슨 뜻이에요?** [누니]　[놉따가]　　　　[뜨시에요]	What does "to have high eyes" mean?

* This is an idiomatic phrase that actually means "to have a high standard."

0327	**'죽을 쑤다'가 무슨 뜻이에요?** [주글]　　　　　　[뜨시에요]	What does "to cook porridge" mean?

* If you use this phrase idiomatically, it can mean "to mess something up."

What does + N + mean?

0328

'눈에 밟히다'가 무슨
[누네] [발피다가]
뜻이에요?
[뜨시에요]

What does "to get stepped on by an eye" mean?

* This is an idiomatic expression that you can use when you cannot get someone or something out of your mind/head.

0329

'호랑이도 제 말 하면 온다'가 무슨 뜻이에요?
[뜨시에요]

What does "even a tiger comes out when people talk about it" mean?

* This is a proverb that means "Speak of the devil."

0330 '인싸'가 무슨 뜻이에요?
[뜨시에요]

What does "in-ssa" mean?

Pattern 031.

| | 은/는 잘 모르겠어요.

0331 그건 **잘 모르겠어요.**
[모르게써요]

I am not sure about that.

* 그건 is short for 그것은.

0332 위치는 **잘 모르겠어요.**
[모르게써요]

I am not sure about the location.

0333 이름은 **잘 모르겠어요.**
[이르믄]   [모르게써요]

I am not sure about its name.

0334 주소는 **잘 모르겠어요.**
[모르게써요]

I am not sure about the address.

0335 이유는 **잘 모르겠어요.**
[모르게써요]

I do not know the reason well.

0336 가격은 **잘 모르겠어요.**
[가겨근]   [모르게써요]

I am not sure about the price.

0337 전화번호는 **잘 모르겠어요.**
[모르게써요]

I am not sure about their phone number.

0338 건물 이름은 **잘 모르겠어요.**
[이르믄]   [모르게써요]

I am not sure about the building name.

I do not know + N + well. / I am not sure about + N.

0339 자세한 내용은 잘 **모르겠어요.**
[모르게써요]

I am not sure about the details.

0340 역까지의 정확한 거리는 잘
[정화칸]
모르겠어요.
[모르게써요]

I am not sure about the exact distance to the station.

0341 엄마 전화번호는 잘 모르겠어요.
[모르게써요]

I am not sure what my mother's phone number is.

Pattern 032.

너무 [-아/어/여] 요.

* If the last syllable of a verb stem has ㅏ or ㅗ, conjugate with -아요. Otherwise,
conjugate it with -어요. Only the verb stems that end with 하 are conjugated with -여요,
and 하여요 is often shortened to 해요.

0342 **너무 짜요.** It is too salty.

0343 **너무 많아요.**
[마나요] It is too much.

0344 **너무 적어요.**
[저:거요] It is too little.

0345 **너무 비싸요.** It is too expensive.

0346 저 **너무** 심심해요. I am so bored.

0347 지금 **너무** 힘들어요.
[힘드러요] I am so tired now.

0348 오늘은 **너무** 바빠요.
[오느른] I am too busy today.

0349 바지가 **너무** 짧아요.
[짤바요] These pants are too short.

It is too + Adj. /
I am so + Adj.

0350 이건 **너무** 어려워**요.**   This is too difficult.

0351 그 카페는 **너무** 시끄러워**요.**   The cafe is too noisy.
[까페는]

0352 이 시험은 **너무** 쉬워**요.**
[시허믄]
This exam is too easy.

Pattern 033.

이게 제일 | -아/어/여 |요.

0353	**이게 제일 짧아요.** [짤바요]	This is the shortest.
0354	**이게 제일 깨끗해요.** [깨끄태요]	This is the cleanest.
0355	**이게 제일 무거워요.**	This is the heaviest.
0356	**이게 제일 맛있어요.** [마시써요]	This is the most delicious.
0357	**이게 제일 싸요.**	This is the cheapest.
0358	**이게 제일 싸고 좋아요.** [조아요]	This is the cheapest and nicest.
0359	**이게 제일 쓰기 편해요.**	This is the easiest to use.
0360	**이게 제일 몸에 나빠요.** [모메]	This is the worst for health.

This is the most + Adj.

0361 **이게 제일** 인기가 없어요.
[인끼가] [업써요]

This is the least popular.

0362 **이게 제일** 인기가 많아요.
[인끼가] [마나요]

This is the most popular.

0363 **이게 제일** 이상해요.
This is the strangest.

Pattern 034.

생각보다 [-아/어/여] 요.

0364
생각보다 작아요.
[생각뽀다]　　[자:가요]

It is smaller than I expected.

0365
생각보다 맛없어요.
[생각뽀다]　　[마덥써요]

It does not taste as good as I expected.

0366
생각보다 간단해요.
[생각뽀다]

It is simpler than I expected.

0367
생각보다 어둡고 불편해요.
[생각뽀다]　　[어둡꼬]

It is darker and more inconvenient than I expected.

0368
생각보다 가볍고 편해요.
[생각뽀다]　　[가볍꼬]

It is lighter and more comfortable than I expected.

0369
생각보다 너무 무거워요.
[생각뽀다]

It is way heavier than I expected.

0370
생각보다 훨씬 가까워요.
[생각뽀다]

It is way closer than I expected.

0371
생각보다 길이가 짧아요.
[생각뽀다]　　[기리가]　　[짤바요]

It is shorter than I expected.

N + is more + Adj + than I expected.

0372
생각보다 거실이 좁아요.
[생각뽀다]　　[거시리]　　[조바요]

The living room is smaller than I expected.

0373
예지 씨는 **생각보다**
[생각뽀다]
똑똑해요.
[똑또캐요]

Yeji is smarter than I expected.

0374
경은 씨는 **생각보다** 착해요.
[생각뽀다]　　[차캐요]
Kyeong-eun is nicer than I expected.

Pattern 035.

뭔가 조금 ☐ -아/어/여 요.

0375 뭔가 조금 부족해요.
[부조캐요]

It is a bit lacking in something.

0376 뭔가 조금 이상해요.

It is a little bit weird.

0377 뭔가 조금 불안해요.
[부란해요]

It is a little bit unsettling.

0378 뭔가 조금 어색해요.
[어새캐요]

It is a little bit awkward.

0379 뭔가 조금 답답해요.
[답따패요]

It is a little bit frustrating.

0380 뭔가 조금 아쉬워요.

It is a little bit disappointing.

0381 뭔가 조금 바보 같아요.
[가타요]

It is a little bit silly.

0382 뭔가 조금 기분 나빠요.

Something about it is a little offensive.

It is a little bit + Adj. / Something about it is a little + Adj.

0383 **뭔가 조금** 빠진 것 같아요.
[껀] [가타요]

It feels like something is missing.

0384 **뭔가 조금** 생각했던 거랑
[생가캗떤]
달라요.

It is a little bit different from what I thought.

0385 그 사람 **뭔가 조금** 수상해요.
Something about him is a little suspicious.

Pattern 036.

지금 [   ] 해요.

* When the verbs that end in -하다 are conjugated with -여요, they become -해요.
** Simple present tense form often takes the place of present progressive form in Korean.

0386	**지금 운동해요.**	I am working out now.
0387	**지금 일해요.**	I am working now.
0388	**지금 빨래해요.**	I am doing laundry now.
0389	**지금 방 청소해요.**	I am tidying up my room now.
0390	**지금 동영상 촬영해요.** [촤령해요]	I am recording a video now.
0391	**지금 책상 정리해요.** [책쌍] [정:니해요]	I am cleaning my desk now.
0392	**지금 친구랑 쇼핑해요.**	I am shopping with my friend now.
0393	**지금 딸이랑 요리해요.** [따리랑]	I am cooking with my daughter now.

I am + V-ing + now.

0394 **지금** 도서관에서 공부**해요.**
[도서과네서]

I am studying at the library now.

0395 **지금** 노래방에서 노래**해요.**

I am singing in a singing room now.

0396 **지금** 도서관에서 게임**해요.**
[도서과네서]　　　[께임해요]

I am playing games at the library now.

Pattern 037.

저는 [ ] 못 해요.

0397	**저는 수영 못 해요.** [모 태요]	I cannot swim.
0398	**저는 영어 못 해요.** [모 태요]	I cannot speak English.
0399	**저는 말 못 해요.** [모 태요]	I cannot tell you.
0400	**저는 거짓말 못 해요.** [거:진말] [모 태요]	I cannot lie.
0401	**저는 그런 거 못 해요.** [모 태요]	I cannot do such a thing.
0402	**저는 혼자서는 못 해요.** [모 태요]	I cannot do it by myself.
0403	**저는 요리 전혀 못 해요.** [모 태요]	I cannot cook at all.
0404	**저는 오늘 출근 못 해요.** [모 태요]	I cannot go to work today.

I cannot + V.

0405 **저는** 석진 씨 포기 **못 해요.**
[석찐]　　　　　[모 태요]

I cannot give up on Seokjin.

0406 **저는** 제임스 씨 이해
[제임쓰]
못 해요.
[모 태요]

I cannot understand James.

0407 **저는** 인터넷 쇼핑 **못 해요.**
[인터넫]　　　　　[모 태요]
I cannot shop online.

Pattern 038.

지금 [　　　　] 고 있어요.

0408	**지금** 아르바이트하**고 있어요.** [이써요]	I am doing my part-time job now.
0409	**지금** 고민하**고 있어요.** [이써요]	I am pondering now.
0410	**지금** 운전하**고 있어요.** [이써요]	I am driving now.
0411	**지금** 알아보**고 있어요.** [아라보고]　　[이써요] .	I am looking into it now.
0412	**지금** 그냥 쉬**고 있어요.** [이써요]	I am just chilling now.
0413	**지금** 거기로 가**고 있어요.** [이써요]	I am heading there now.
0414	**지금** 다이어트 하**고 있어요.** [이써요]	I am on a diet now.
0415	**지금** 이메일 쓰**고 있어요.** [이써요]	I am writing an email now.

I am + V-ing + now.

0416 **지금 휴대폰 고르고 있어요.**
[이써요]

I am choosing a phone now.

0417 **지금 두 사람이 이야기하고**
[사:라미]
있어요.
[이써요]

The two people are talking to each other now.

0418 **지금 우주선을 타고 있어요.**
[우주서늘]　　　　[이써요]

I am riding on a spaceship now.

Pattern 039.

아직 [-는] 중이에요.

* Attach -는 to a verb stem. Nouns can be used without any particle.

0419 **아직** 생각 **중이에요.**   I am still thinking.

0420 **아직** 고민 **중이에요.**   I am still pondering.

0421 **아직** 계획 **중이에요.**   I am still planning.

0422 **아직** 휴가 **중이에요.**   I am still in the middle of vacation.

0423 **아직** 통화 **중이에요.**   I am still talking on the phone.

0424 **아직** 이탈리아 여행 **중이에요.**   I am still traveling Italy.

0425 **아직** 경화 씨랑 의논 **중이에요.**   I am still discussing it with Kyung-hwa.

0426 **아직** 얘기하는 **중이에요.**   We are still talking.

I am still + V-ing. /
I am still in the middle of + N.

0427 **아직** 기다리는 **중이에요.** I am still waiting.

0428 **아직** 드라마 보는
중이에요. I am still watching the drama.

0429 **아직** 도망가는 **중이에요.**
I am still in the middle of running
away.

Pattern 040.

[ ] 고 싶어요.

0430 쉬고 **싶어요.**
[시퍼요]

I want to get some rest.

0431 일하고 **싶어요.**
[시퍼요]

I want to work.

0432 그만하고 **싶어요.**
[시퍼요]

I want to quit.

0433 한국어 배우고 **싶어요.**
[한:구거]　　　　　[시퍼요]

I want to learn Korean.

0434 집에 가고 **싶어요.**
[지베]　　　　[시퍼요]

I want to go home.

0435 혼자 쉬고 **싶어요.**
[시퍼요]

I want to get some rest alone.

0436 더 연습하고 **싶어요.**
[연스파고]　　[시퍼요]

I want to practice more.

0437 선생님이 되고 **싶어요.**
[선생니미]　　　　[시퍼요]

I want to be a teacher.

I want to + V.

0438 좋은 엄마가 되고 **싶어요.**
[조은]　　　　　　　[시퍼요]

I want to be a good mom.

0439 이모랑 같이 놀고 **싶어요.**
　　　[가치]　　　[시퍼요]

I want to hang out with my aunt.

0440 순간 이동 하고 **싶어요.**
　　　　　　　　[시퍼요]

I want to teleport.

Pattern 041.

뭐 [   ]고 싶어요?

0441	**뭐 하고 싶어요?** [시퍼요]	What do you want to do?
0442	**뭐 보고 싶어요?** [시퍼요]	What do you want to see?
0443	**뭐 먹고 싶어요?** [먹꼬] [시퍼요]	What do you want to eat?
0444	**뭐 사고 싶어요?** [시퍼요]	What do you want to buy?
0445	**뭐 그리고 싶어요?** [시퍼요]	What do you want to draw?
0446	**뭐 만들고 싶어요?** [시퍼요]	What do you want to make?
0447	**뭐 배우고 싶어요?** [시퍼요]	What do you want to learn?
0448	**뭐 먼저 하고 싶어요?** [시퍼요]	What do you want to do first?

What do you want to + V?

0449 **뭐 먼저 바꾸고 싶어요?**
[시퍼요]

What do you want to change first?

0450 **가장 먼저 뭐 하고 싶어요?**
[시퍼요]

What do you want to do before anything else?

0451 **복권 당첨되면 뭐 하고 싶어요?**
[복꿘]   [시퍼요]

If you win the lottery, what do you want to do?

Pattern 042.

(으)세요.

* Attach -으세요 to a verb stem that ends with a consonant. Otherwise, attach -세요.

0452 **앉으세요.**
[안즈세요]
Please take a seat.

0453 **들어오세요.**
[드러오세요]
Please come on in.

0454 **조심하세요.**
Please be careful.

0455 **서두르세요.**
Please hurry.

0456 **이거 주세요.**
Please give it to me.

0457 **이거 쓰세요.**
Please use this one.

0458 **많이 드세요.**
[마:니]
Please help yourself.

0459 **여기에서 기다리세요.**
Please wait here.

Please + V.

0460 **직접 보세요.**
[직쩝]

Please take a look yourself.

0461 **처음부터 다시 하세요.**

Please do it all over again.

0462 **비키세요.**
Please get out of my way.

Pattern 043.

빨리 [   ] (으)세요.

0463 **빨리 하세요.**　　　　　　Hurry up and do it.

0464 **빨리 오세요.**　　　　　　Hurry up and come here.

0465 **빨리 나으세요.**　　　　　Feel better soon.

* Here, -으세요 is attached because "to feel/get better" in Korean is 낫다, whose verb stem ends in a consonant. It is one of the verbs that are conjugated irregularly, so the ㅅ is dropped.

0466 **빨리 잊으세요.**
　　　[이즈세요]　　　　　　Please forget it.

0467 **빨리 돌아오세요.**
　　　[도라오세요]　　　　　Please come back quickly.

0468 **빨리 준비하세요.**　　　　Please get ready quickly.

0469 **빨리 집에 가세요.**
　　　[지베]　　　　　　　　Please go home quickly.

0470 **빨리 숙제 끝내세요.**
　　　[숙쩨] [끈내세요]　　　Hurry up and finish your homework.

Hurry up and + V. /
Please + V + quickly.

0471 **빨리** 저 좀 보세요.　　Please look at me now.

0472 **빨리** 여기서 나가세요.　　Hurry up and get out of here.

0473 **빨리** 도망가세요.
Hurry up and run away.

Pattern 044.

이쪽으로 [ ] (으)세요.

0474 **이쪽으로 오세요.**
[이쪼그로]

Please come this way.

0475 **이쪽으로 들어가세요.**
[이쪼그로]　[드러가세요]

Please use this entrance.

0476 **이쪽으로 모이세요.**
[이쪼그로]

Everyone, please come here.

0477 **이쪽으로 앉으세요.**
[이쪼그로]　[안즈세요]

Please take a seat here.

0478 **이쪽으로 주차하세요.**
[이쪼그로]

Please park here.

0479 **이쪽으로 올라오세요.**
[이쪼그로]

Please come up this way.

0480 **이쪽으로 옮기세요.**
[이쪼그로]　[옴기세요]

Please move it here.

0481 **이쪽으로 내려가세요.**
[이쪼그로]

Please go down this way.

Please + V + this way.

0482 **이쪽으로 저를 따라오세요.**
[이쪼그로]
Please follow me this way.

0483 **이쪽으로 천천히 걸어오세요.**
[이쪼그로]　　　　　[거러오세요]
Please walk this way slowly.

0484 **이쪽으로 숨으세요.**
[이쪼그로]　　　[수므세요]
Please hide this way.

Pattern 045.

지 마세요.

0485	하**지 마세요.**	Do not do that.
0486	가**지 마세요.**	Do not go.
0487	낙서하**지 마세요.** [낙써하지]	Do not scribble.
0488	만지**지 마세요.**	Do not touch.
0489	포기하**지 마세요.**	Do not give up.
0490	고민하**지 마세요.**	Do not think too much.
0491	미안해하**지 마세요.**	Do not be sorry.
0492	소리 지르**지 마세요.**	Do not shout.

Do not + V.

0493 **그렇게 생각하지 마세요.**
[그러케] [생가카지]

Do not think that way.

0494 **아직 들어가지 마세요.**
[드러가지]

Do not enter yet.

0495 **저 너무 좋아하지 마세요.**
[조아하지]

Do not like me too much.

Pattern 046.

왜 그렇게 ┃ -아/어/여 ┃요?

0496	왜 그렇게 생각해요? [그러케]　[생가캐요]	Why do you think so?
0497	왜 그렇게 웃어요? [그러케]　[우서요]	Why do you smile like that?
0498	왜 그렇게 쳐다봐요? [그러케]　[처:다봐요]	Why do you stare at me like that?
0499	왜 그렇게 걱정해요? [그러케]　[걱쩡해요]	Why do you worry so much?
0500	왜 그렇게 크게 말해요? [그러케]	Why do you talk so loud?
0501	왜 그렇게 천천히 걸어요? [그러케]　　　　[거러요]	Why do you walk so slowly?
0502	왜 그렇게 빨리 걸어요? [그러케]　　　[거러요]	Why do you walk so fast?
0503	왜 그렇게 당근을 싫어해요? [그러케]　[당그늘]　[시러해요]	Why do you hate carrots so much?

Why do you + V + like that?

0504 **왜 그렇게 커피를 많이**
　　[그러케]　　　　　[마:니]
마셔요?

Why do you drink coffee so much?

0505 **왜 그렇게 밥을 조금**
　　[그러케]　[바블]
먹어요?
　[머거요]

Why do you eat so little?

0506 **왜 그렇게 밥을 빨리 먹어요?**
　　[그러케]　[바블]　　　[머거요]
Why do you eat so fast?

Pattern 047.

이거 어디에서 | -아/어/여 | 써어요?

* If the last syllable of a verb stem has ㅏ or ㅗ, conjugate it with -았어요. Otherwise, conjugate it with -었어요. Only the verb stems that end with 하 are conjugated with -였어요, and 하였어요 is often shortened to 했어요.

0507	**이거 어디에서 샀어요?** [사써요]	Where did you buy this?
0508	**이거 어디에서 났어요?** [나써요]	Where did you get this?
0509	**이거 어디에서 주문했어요?** [주문해써요]	Where did you order this?
0510	**이거 어디에서 봤어요?** [바써요]	Where did you see this?
0511	**이거 어디에서 찾았어요?** [차자써요]	Where did you find this?
0512	**이거 어디에서 찍었어요?** [찌거써요]	Where did you take this (photo/video)?
0513	**이거 어디에서 고쳤어요?** [고처써요]	Where did you get this fixed?
0514	**이거 어디에서 가져왔어요?** [가저와써요]	Where did you take this from?

Where did you + V + this?

0515 **이거 어디에서 만들었어요?**
[만드러써요]

Where did you make this?

0516 **이거 어디에서 촬영했어요?**
[촤령해써요]

Where did you film this?

* 찍다 and 촬영하다 mean the same thing, but 촬영하다 is more formal.

0517 **이거 어디에서 다운 받았어요?**
[따운] [바다써요]
Where did you download this?

Pattern 048.

벌써 [-아/어/여] 쓰어요.

0518	**벌써 끝났어요.** [끈나써요]	It has already finished.
0519	**벌써 말했어요.** [말해써요]	I already told (someone).
0520	**벌써 도착했어요.** [도차캐써요]	It has already arrived.
0521	**벌써 다 했어요.** [해써요]	I have already finished.
0522	**벌써 다 먹었어요.** [머거써요]	I have already finished the food.
0523	**벌써 다 나았어요.** [나아써요]	I have already recovered.
0524	**벌써 다 마셨어요.** [마셔써요]	I have already drunk it all.
0525	**벌써 영화 시작했어요.** [시자캐써요]	The movie already started.

I already + V-ed. /
It has already + V-ed.

0526 **벌써** 방 청소 다 **했어요.**
[해써요]

I have already cleaned my room.

0527 **벌써** 다른 동네로 이사 **갔어요.**
[가써요]

They have already moved to another town.

0528 **벌써** 제가 소문**냈어요.**
[소문내써요]

I already spread the rumor.

Pattern 049.

아직 안 [-아/어/여] 써어요.

0529
아직 안 봤어요.
[봐써요]

I have not seen it yet.

0530
아직 안 정했어요.
[정해써요]

I have not decided yet.

0531
아직 안 먹었어요.
[머거써요]

I have not eaten yet.

0532
아직 안 시켰어요.
[시켜써요]

I have not ordered it yet.

0533
아직 안 해 봤어요.
[봐써요]

I have not tried yet.

0534
아직 안 알아봤어요.
[아라봐써요]

I have not looked into it yet.

0535
음식 아직 안 왔어요.
[와써요]

The food has not arrived yet.

* Unless you pause between 안 and 왔어요, 안 왔어요 is usually pronounced as [아 놔써요].

0536
아직 목욕 안 했어요.
[모곡]   [해써요]

I have not taken a bath yet.

I have not + V-ed + yet.

0537 **아직** 거기까지 **안 읽었어요.**
[일거써요]

I have not read that far yet.

* If you say "안 읽었어요" without pausing between 안 and 읽었어요, it is pronounced as [아 닐거써요]. Also, if you regard it as one word, it can be pronounced as [안닐거써요].

아직 석진 씨한테
[석찐]

0538 **안 물어봤어요.**
[무러봐써요]

I have not asked Seokjin yet.

0539 **아직** 돈 **안 냈어요.**
[내써요]

You have not paid money yet.

Pattern 050.

어쩌다가 | -아/어/여 | 쓰어요?

0540 어쩌다가 그랬어요?
[그래써요]
How did it happen?

0541 어쩌다가 넘어졌어요?
[너머저써요]
How did you fall down?

0542 어쩌다가 다쳤어요?
[다처써요]
How did you get hurt?

0543 어쩌다가 2층에서
[이층에서]
떨어졌어요?
[떠러저써요]
How did you fall from the second floor?

0544 어쩌다가 이렇게 됐어요?
[이러케]   [돼써요]
How did it turn out to be like this?

0545 어쩌다가 길을 잃었어요?
[기를]   [이러써요]
How did you get lost?

0546 어쩌다가 멍이 들었어요?
[드러써요]
How did you get bruised?

0547 어쩌다가 핸드폰을
[핸드포늘]
잃어버렸어요?
[이러버려써요]
How did you lose your phone?

How did you + V?

0548 **어쩌다가** 커피를 바지에 쏟았어요?
[쏘다써요]

How did you spill coffee on your pants?

0549 **어쩌다가** 한국에 오게
[한:구게]
됐어요?
[돼써요]

How did you get to come to Korea?

0550 **어쩌다가** 뉴스에 나왔어요?
[뉴쓰에]　[나와써요]
How did you end up in the news?

Pattern 051.

저는 아무것도 안 $\boxed{-\text{아/어/여}}$ 썼어요.

0551 저는 아무것도 안 했어요.
[아:무걷또] [해써요]
I did not do anything.

0552 저는 아무것도 안 만졌어요.
[아:무걷또] [만저써요]
I did not touch anything.

0553 저는 아무것도 안 먹었어요.
[아:무걷또] [머거써요]
I did not eat anything.

0554 저는 아무것도 안 바꿨어요.
[아:무걷또] [바꿔써요]
I did not change anything.

0555 저는 아무것도 안 샀어요.
[아:무걷또] [사써요]
I did not buy anything.

0556 저는 아무것도 안 틀렸어요.
[아:무걷또] [틀려써요]
I did not get anything wrong.

0557 저는 아무것도 안 시켰어요.
[아:무걷또] [시켜써요]
I did not order anything.

0558 저는 아무것도 안 마셨어요.
[아:무걷또] [마셔써요]
I did not drink anything.

I did not + V + anything.

0559 **저는 아무것도 안 눌렀어요.**
[아ː무걷또] [눌러써요]

I did not press anything.

0560 **저는 아무것도 안**
[아ː무걷또]
건드렸어요.
[건드려써요]

I did not touch anything.

* 건드리다 only implies that one puts their hand onto something slightly, whereas 만지다 can also refer to touching by grasping something or picking it up.

0561 **저는 아무것도 안 가져왔어요.**
[아ː무걷또] [가저와써요]

I did not bring anything.

Pattern 052.

-아 주세요.

* If the last syllable of a verb stem either has ㅏ or ㅗ, conjugate it with -아 주세요. If the verb stem ends in ㅏ without a final consonant (받침), however, just add 주세요.

0562 안아 **주세요.**
[아나]

Please hug me.

0563 올라가 **주세요.**

Please go up.

0564 사 **주세요.**

Please buy it (for me).

0565 손을 잡아 **주세요.**
[소늘] [자바]

Please hold my hand.

0566 답을 골라 **주세요.**
[다블]

Please choose the answer.

0567 이쪽으로 와 **주세요.**
[이쪼그로]

Please come over here.

0568 여기로 가 **주세요.**

Please go this way.

0569 제 핸드폰 찾아 **주세요.**
[차자]

Please find my phone.

Please + V (+ for me).

0570 **하지 말아 주세요.**
[마라]
Please do not do it.

* When you want to say "Please do not + V", you can use "V + -지 말아 주세요".

0571 **잊지 말아 주세요.**
[읻찌]　[마라]
Please do not forget.

0572 저 차 따라가 **주세요.**
Please follow that car.

Pattern 053.

☐ -어 주세요.

* If the last syllable of a verb stem does not have ㅏ or ㅗ, conjugate it with -어 주세요.

0573 읽어 **주세요.**
[일거]

Please read it for me.

0574 만들어 **주세요.**
[만드러]

Please make it for me.

0575 기다려 **주세요.**

Please wait.

0576 가르쳐 **주세요.**
[가르처]

Please teach me.

0577 저도 알려 **주세요.**

Please let me know too.

0578 사진 보여 **주세요.**

Please show me the picture.

0579 약속을 지켜 **주세요.**
[약쏘글]

Please keep your promise.

0580 조금만 남겨 **주세요.**

Please leave some for me.

Please + V (+ for me).

0581 작은 사이즈로 바꿔 **주세요.**
[자:근] [싸이즈로]

Please change it for a smaller size.

0582 후추 많이 넣어 **주세요.**
[마:니] [너어]

Please put a lot of pepper.

0583 비켜 **주세요.**
Please get out of my way.

Pattern 054.

해 주세요.

* When -하다 is conjugated with -여 주세요, it becomes -해 주세요.

0584 주문**해 주세요.** Please make an order.

0585 사랑**해 주세요.** Please love me.

0586 이해**해 주세요.** Please understand.

0587 조심**해 주세요.** Please be careful.

0588 함께 축하**해 주세요.** Please celebrate together.
[추카해]

0589 크게 말**해 주세요.** Please speak louder.

0590 앞으로 이동**해 주세요.** Please move forward.
[아프로]

0591 사진을 확인**해 주세요.** Please check the photo.
[사지늘]   [화긴해]

Please + V (+ for me).

0592 고양이를 구해 **주세요.**   Please save the cat.

0593 메뉴를 추천**해 주세요.**   Please recommend a dish.

0594 저부터 구해 **주세요.**
Please save me first.

Pattern 055.

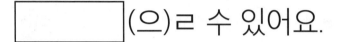

□□□□ (으)ㄹ 수 있어요.

* Attach -을 to a verb stem that ends in a consonant. Otherwise, attach -ㄹ.

0595 **갈 수 있어요.**
[갈 쑤] [이써요]

I can go.

0596 **할 수 있어요.**
[할 쑤] [이써요]

I can do it.

0597 **읽을 수 있어요.**
[일글 쑤]   [이써요]

I can read.

0598 **설명할 수 있어요.**
[설명할 쑤]   [이써요]

I can explain.

0599 **크게 말할 수 있어요.**
          [말할 쑤]   [이써요]

I can speak out loud.

0600 **일찍 일어날 수 있어요.**
          [이러날 쑤]   [이써요]

I can get up early.

0601 **빨리 끝낼 수 있어요.**
          [끈낼 쑤]   [이써요]

I can finish it quickly.

0602 **저녁에 만날 수 있어요.**
[저녀게]   [만날 쑤]   [이써요]

I can meet (you) in the evening.

I can + V.

0603 **다 먹을 수 있어요.**
[머글 쑤]　　[이써요]

I can eat it all.

0604 **저 혼자 할 수 있어요.**
　　　　[할 쑤]　[이써요]

I can do it by myself.

0605 **도망갈 수 있어요.**
[도망갈 쑤]　　　[이써요]
I can run away.

Pattern 056.

☐ -아 야 돼요.

* If the last syllable of a verb stem either has ㅏ or ㅗ, conjugate it with -아야. If the verb stem ends in ㅏ without a final consonant (받침), however, just add -야 돼요.

0606 **사야 돼요.**　　　I should buy it.

0607 **가야 돼요.**　　　I have to go.

0608 **만나야 돼요.**　　　I have to meet (someone).

0609 **지금 나가야 돼요.**　　　I have to go out now.

0610 **드라마 봐야 돼요.**　　　I have to watch a drama.

0611 **새 휴대폰을 사야 돼요.**
[휴대포늘]　　　I should buy a new phone.

0612 **10시까지 와야 돼요.**
[열씨까지]　　　You should come by 10.

0613 **친구한테 물어봐야 돼요.**
[무러봐야]　　　I should ask my friend.

I have to + V. / I should + V.

0614	아침 일찍 일어나**야 돼요.** [이러나야]

I have to get up early in the morning.

0615	저기서 친구를 만나**야** **돼요.**

I am supposed to meet my friends over there.

> 0616 저희 행성으로 돌아가**야 돼요.**
> [저히]   [도라가야]
>
> I have to go back to my planet.

Pattern 057.

☐ -어야 돼요.

* If the last syllable of a verb stem does not have ㅏ or ㅗ, conjugate it with -어야.

| 0617 | 쉬어**야 돼요.** | I should get some rest. |

| 0618 | 믿어**야 돼요.**
[미더야] | I have to believe it. |

| 0619 | 걸어**야 돼요.**
[거러야] | I have to walk. |

| 0620 | 기다려**야 돼요.** | I should wait. |

| 0621 | 약을 먹어**야 돼요.**
[야글] [머거야] | I have to take medicine. |

| 0622 | 한국어를 배워**야 돼요.**
[한:구거를] | I have to learn Korean. |

| 0623 | 직접 만들어**야 돼요.**
[직쩝] [만드러야] | I should make it myself. |

| 0624 | 가만히 있어**야 돼요.**
[이써야] | You should stay still. |

I have to + V. / I should + V.

0625 **신문을 매일 읽어야 돼요.**
[신무늘]　　　[일거야]

I should read the newspaper every day.

0626 **먼저 뚜껑을 열어야 돼요.**
　　　　　[여러야]

You should open the lid first.

한 달 동안 김밥만 먹어야 돼요.
0627　　　[김빰만]　　[머거야]

I have to eat only kimbap for one month.

* People often say "time period + 동안" as one word, which is why 동안 is often pronounced as [똥안].

Pattern 058.

 해야 돼요.

* When -하다 is conjugated with -여야, it becomes -해야.

0628	기억**해야 돼요.** [기어캐야]	I have to remember.
0629	사과**해야 돼요.**	I have to apologize.
0630	연락**해야 돼요.** [열라캐야]	I have to contact (someone).
0631	빨리 **해야 돼요.**	I have to do it quickly.
0632	조용히 **해야 돼요.**	We should be quiet.
0633	솔직히 말**해야 돼요.** [솔찌키]	I should tell (someone) frankly.
0634	좀 더 생각**해야 돼요.** [생가캐야]	I need to think about it more.
0635	당장 시작**해야 돼요.** [시자캐야]	I have to start it right now.

I have to + V. / I should + V.

0636 이거 먼저 **해야 돼요.** I have to do this first.

0637 다른 거 먼저 **해야 돼요.** I have to do other things first.

0638 제 보디가드를 **구해야 돼요.**
I have to save my bodyguard.
* 구하다 can also mean "to look for", so it can also
mean "I have to look for my bodyguard."

139

Pattern 059.

언제까지 [-아/어/여] 야 돼요?

0639 **언제까지 기다려야 돼요?**   How long should I wait?

0640 **언제까지 돌아와야 돼요?**
[도라와야]   When should I come back by?

0641 **언제까지 돌려줘야 돼요?**   When should I return it by?

0642 **언제까지 끝내야 돼요?**
[끈내야]   When should I finish it by?

0643 **언제까지 다 해야 돼요?**   When should I get it done by?

0644 **언제까지 여기 있어야 돼요?**
[이써야]   How long should I stay here?

0645 **언제까지 들고 있어야 돼요?**
[이써야]   How long should I hold it?

0646 **언제까지 서 있어야 돼요?**
[이써야]   How long should I stand up?

Until/By when should I + V?/ How long should I + V?

TRACK 059

0647 **언제까지 다이어트 해야 돼요?**　　How long should I be on a diet?

0648 **언제까지 죽만 먹어야 돼요?**　　Until when do I have to only eat porridge?
[중만] [머거야]

0649 **언제까지 참아야 돼요?**
[차마야]
How long should I bear it?

141

Pattern 060.

☐ (으)ㄹ 거예요.

0650 **집에 갈 거예요.**
[지베] [갈 꺼예요]

I am going home.

0651 **쉴 거예요.**
[쉴 꺼예요]

I am going to get some rest.

0652 **운동할 거예요.**
[운동할 꺼예요]

I am going to work out.

0653 **공부할 거예요.**
[공부할 꺼예요]

I am going to study.

0654 **친구 만날 거예요.**
[만날 꺼예요]

I am going to meet my friend.

0655 **영화 볼 거예요.**
[볼 꺼예요]

I am going to see a movie.

0656 **조카한테 선물로 줄 거예요.**
[줄 꺼예요]

I am going to give it to my niece as a gift.

0657 **하루 종일 책 읽을 거예요.**
[일글 꺼예요]

I am going to read books all day long.

I am going to + V.

0658 **예지 씨랑 같이 먹을 거예요.**
[가치] [머글 꺼예요]

I am going to eat together with Yeji.

0659 **내일 다시 시작할 거예요.**
[시자칼 꺼예요]

I am going to start over tomorrow.

0660 **세상을 구할 거예요.**
[구할 꺼예요]

I am going to save the world.

Pattern 061.

언제 [   ] (으)ㄹ 거예요?

0661 **언제 살 거예요?**
[살 꺼예요]
When will you buy it?

0662 **언제 할 거예요?**
[할 꺼예요]
When will you do it?

0663 **언제 끝낼 거예요?**
[끈낼 꺼예요]
When will you finish it?

0664 **언제 시작할 거예요?**
[시자칼 꺼예요]
When will you start?

0665 **언제 출발할 거예요?**
[출발할 꺼예요]
When will you depart?

0666 **친구들 언제 만날 거예요?**
[만날 꺼예요]
When will you meet your friends?

0667 **도서관에 언제 갈 거예요?**
[도서과네]   [갈 꺼예요]
When will you go to the library?

0668 **제인 씨한테 언제 말할 거예요?**
[말할 꺼예요]
When will you tell Jane?

When will you + V?

0669 자전거는 **언제 고칠 거예요?**
[고칠 꺼예요]

When will you fix the bicycle?

0670 저녁 식사는 **언제**
[식싸는]
준비할 거예요?
[준비할 꺼예요]

When will you prepare dinner?

0671 **언제** 비킬 **거예요?**
[비킬 꺼예요]
When will you get out of the way?

Pattern 062.

☐고 올게요.

0672 설거지하고 **올게요.**
[올께요]

I will be back after washing the dishes.

0673 밥 먹고 **올게요.**
[밤 먹꼬] [올께요]

I will be back after having a meal.

0674 점심 먹고 **올게요.**
[먹꼬] [올께요]

I will be back after having lunch.

0675 전화 좀 하고 **올게요.**
[올께요]

I will be back after making a call.

0676 잠깐 통화하고 **올게요.**
[올께요]

I will be back in a moment after taking this call.

0677 10분만 쉬고 **올게요.**
[십뿐만] [올께요]

I will be back after taking a 10-minute break.

0678 좀 더 둘러보고 **올게요.**
[올께요]

I will be back after browsing.

0679 현우 씨한테 물어보고 **올게요.**
[허누] [무러보고] [올께요]

I will be back after asking Hyunwoo.

I will be back after + V-ing.

0680 도서관에서 공부하고 **올게요.**
[도서과네서] [올께요]

I will be back after studying in the library.

0681 주연 씨 좀 도와주고 **올게요.**
[올께요]

I will be back after helping out Jooyeon.

0682 잠깐 기자 회견 하고 **올게요.**
[올께요]

I will be back after a short press conference.

Pattern 063.

잠깐만 ⬚ (으)ㄹ게요.

* Attach -을게요 to a verb stem that ends in a consonant. Otherwise, attach -ㄹ게요.

0683	**잠깐만 쉴게요.** [쉴께요]	I will get some rest for just a little while.
0684	**잠깐만 쓸게요.** [쓸께요]	I will use it for just a little while.
0685	**잠깐만 여기 앉을게요.** [안즐께요]	I will sit here for just a little while.
0686	**잠깐만 생각해 볼게요.** [생가캐]　[볼께요]	I will think about it for just a little while.
0687	**잠깐만 나갔다 올게요.** [나갇따]　[올께요]	I will go outside for just a little while and come back.
0688	**잠깐만 화장실 다녀올게요.** [다녀올께요]	I will stop by the restroom for just a little while.
0689	**잠깐만 편의점에** [펴늬저메/펴니저메] **갔다 올게요.** [갇따]　[올께요]	I will go to the convenience store for just a little while and come back.

* 다녀오다 and 갔다 오다 mean the same thing. There is no space 다녀오다 becaue it is one word, whereas there is a space in the middle of 갔다 오다 because it is a phrase; a combination of two words.

I will + V + for just a little while. /
Let me + V + for just a little while.

0690 **잠깐만** 통화 좀 **할게요.**
[할께요]

I will be talking on the phone for just a little while.

0691 **잠깐만** 주연 씨랑 얘기 좀 **할게요.**
[할께요]

I will talk to Jooyeon for just a little while.

0692 **잠깐만** 친구 만나고 **올게요.**
[올께요]

I will meet my friend for just a little while and come back.

0693 **잠깐만** 비웃을게요.
[비:우슬께요]

Let me laugh at you for just a little bit.

Pattern 064.

그러면 우리 [   ](으)ㄹ까요?

* Attach -을까요? to a verb stem that ends with a consonant. Otherwise, attach -ㄹ까요?

0694 **그러면 우리 시작할까요?**
[시자칼까요]
Then, shall we start?

0695 **그러면 우리 앉을까요?**
[안즐까요]
Then, shall we take a seat?

0696 **그러면 우리 이렇게 할까요?**
[이러케]
Then, shall we do it this way?

0697 **그러면 우리 어떻게 할까요?**
[어떠케]
Then, how shall we do it?

0698 **그러면 우리 뭐 할까요?**
Then, what shall we do?

0699 **그러면 우리 지금 갈까요?**
Then, shall we go now?

0700 **그러면 우리 저기 가 볼까요?**
Then, shall we check out that place?

0701 **그러면 우리 같이 여행 갈까요?**
[가치]
Then, shall we go on a trip together?

Then, shall we + V?

0702 그러면 우리 불고기 먹을까요?
[머글까요]

Then, shall we eat bulgogi?

0703 그러면 우리 현우 씨한테
[현누]
물어볼까요?
[무러볼까요]

Then, shall we ask Hyunwoo?

0704 그러면 우리 내일 결혼할까요?
Then, shall we get married tomorrow?

Pattern 065.

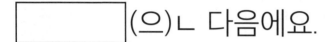

(으)ㄴ 다음에요.

* Attach -은 to a verb stem that ends with a consonant. Otherwise, attach -ㄴ.

0705 물어본 **다음에요.**
[무러본] [다으메요]

After asking.

0706 다 먹은 **다음에요.**
[머근] [다으메요]

After eating it all.

0707 이거 끝낸 **다음에요.**
[끈낸] [다으메요]

After finishing this.

0708 숙제 다 한 **다음에요.**
[숙쩨] [다으메요]

After finishing my homework.

0709 숙제부터 한 **다음에요.**
[숙쩨부터] [다으메요]

After finishing my homework first.

0710 일부터 끝낸 **다음에요.**
[끈낸] [다으메요]

After getting work done first.

0711 화장부터 한 **다음에요.**
[다으메요]

After putting on makeup first.

0712 메뉴부터 고른 **다음에요.**
[다으메요]

After choosing dishes first.

After + V-ing. /
Only after + V-ing.

0713 석진 씨가 확인한 **다음에요.**
[석찐] [화긴한] [다으메요]

After Seokjin checks.

0714 캐시 씨가 도착한 **다음에요.**
[캐씨] [도차칸] [다으메요]

After Cassie arrives.

0715 화장실 갔다 온 **다음에요.**
[갇따] [다으메요]

After I use the bathroom.

Pattern 066.

[⬚] (으)ㄴ 것 같아요.

0716	**포기한 것 같아요.** [건] [가타요]	I think they gave up.
0717	**준비된 것 같아요.** [건] [가타요]	I think it is ready.
0718	**고장 난 것 같아요.** [건] [가타요]	I think it is broken.
0719	**캐시 씨가 이긴 것 같아요.** [캐씨] [건] [가타요]	I think Cassie won.
0720	**제가 오해한 것 같아요.** [건] [가타요]	I think I misunderstood.
0721	**그건 이미 산 것 같아요.** [건] [가타요]	I think we already bought it.
0722	**어디서 본 것 같아요.** [건] [가타요]	I think I have seen it somewhere.
0723	**너무 많이 받은 것 같아요.** [마니] [바든] [건] [가타요]	I think I received it too much.

I think + S + V-ed.

0724 실수로 두 번 누른 **것 같아요.**
[실쑤로] [걷] [가타요]

I think I mistakenly pressed it two times.

0725 현우 씨는 먼저 간 **것 같아요.**
[허누] [걷] [가타요]

I think Hyunwoo left earlier.

0726 제가 먹은 **것 같아요.**
[머근] [걷] [가타요]

I think I ate it.

Pattern 067.

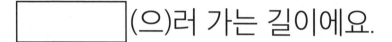 (으)러 가는 길이에요.

* Use -러 가는 길이에요 when a verb stem ends in a vowel. Otherwise, use -으러 가는 길이에요.

0727 운동하**러 가는 길이에요.**
[기리에요]
I am on my way to go and work out.

0728 공부하**러 가는 길이에요.**
[기리에요]
I am on my way to go and study.

0729 일하**러 가는 길이에요.**
[기리에요]
I am on my way to go and work.

0730 밥 먹**으러 가는 길이에요.**
[밤 머그러]　　　　[기리에요]
I am on my way to go and have a meal.

0731 기차 타**러 가는 길이에요.**
[기리에요]
I am on my way to go and get on the train.

0732 친구 만나**러 가는 길이에요.**
[기리에요]
I am on my way to go and meet up with my friend.

0733 커피 마시**러 가는 길이에요.**
[기리에요]
I am on my way to go and get some coffee.

0734 춤 연습하**러 가는 길이에요.**
[연스파러]　　　　[기리에요]
I am on my way to go and practice dancing.

I am on my way to go and + V.

0735 백화점에 쇼핑하러 가는
[배콰저메]
길이에요.
[기리에요]

I am on my way to go shopping in a department store.

0736 제주도에 여행하러 가는
길이에요.
[기리에요]

I am on my way to go traveling in Jeju Island.

0737 친구랑 싸우러 가는 길이에요.
[기리에요]

I am on my way to go and fight with my friend.

Pattern 068.

( )시쯤에 ⬚ (으)ㄹ 거예요.

* Use native Korean numbers when you say the hour.

0738
12시쯤에 전화할 거예요.
[열뚜시쯔메] [전:화할 꺼예요]

They will call me at around 12.

0739
8시쯤에 끝날 거예요.
[여덜씨쯔메] [끈날 꺼예요]

It will be over at around 8.

0740
10시쯤에 집에 갈 거예요.
[열씨쯔메] [지베] [갈 꺼예요]

I will go home at around 10.

0741
2시쯤에 친구 만날 거예요.
[두시쯔메] [만날 꺼예요]

I will meet my friend at around 2.

0742
6시쯤에 종이 울릴 거예요.
[여섯씨쯔메] [울릴 꺼예요]

The bell will ring at around 6.

0743
4시쯤에 택배가 올 거예요.
[네시쯔메] [택빼가] [올 꺼예요]

A parcel will be delivered at around 4.

0744
3시쯤에 드라마
[세시쯔메]
시작할 거예요.
[시자칼 꺼예요]

The drama will start at around 3.

0745
11시쯤에 영어 수업이
[열한시쯔메] [수어비]
끝날 거예요.
[끈날 꺼예요]

My English class will be over at around 11.

S + will + V + at around
( ) o'clock.

0746
7시쯤에 밥 먹으러 갈 거예요.
[일곱씨쯔메] [밥 머그러]　　[갈 꺼예요]

I will go eat at around 7.

0747
1시쯤에 엄마가 데리러
[한시쯔메]
올 거예요.
[올 꺼예요]

My mom will come to pick me up at around 1.

0748
새벽 3시쯤에 일어날 거예요.
[세시쯔메]　　[이러날 꺼예요]
I will wake up at around 3 am.

Pattern 069.

-아/어/여 도 돼요.

* If the last syllable of a verb stem has ㅏ or ㅗ, conjugate it with -아도 돼요. Otherwise, conjugate it with -어도 돼요. Only the verb stems that end with 하 are conjugated with -여도 돼요, and 하여도 돼요 is often shortened to 해도 돼요.

0749	**가도 돼요.**	You may leave.
0750	**자도 돼요.**	You may go to bed.
0751	**먹어도 돼요.** [머거도]	You may eat.
0752	**좀 늦어도 돼요.** [느저도]	It is okay to be late.
0753	**더 시켜도 돼요.**	It is okay to order more.
0754	**내일 해도 돼요.**	It is okay to do it tomorrow.
0755	**먼저 들어가도 돼요.** [드러가도]	It is okay to go in first.
0756	**천천히 골라도 돼요.**	It is okay to take your time choosing.

You may + V. /
It is okay to + V.

0757 인터넷에서 사도 **돼요.**
[인터네세서]

It is okay to buy it online.

0758 지금 안 해도 **돼요.**

You do not have to do that now.

* "안 -아/어/여도 돼요" means "You do not have to + V" rather than "You may not + V" or "It is not okay to + V."

0759 이거 다 부숴도 **돼요.**
You may smash all of this.

Pattern 070.

-아/어/여 도 돼요?

0760 시작해도 돼요?
[시자캐도]

Can I start?

0761 그만해도 돼요?

Can I stop doing this?

0762 집에 가도 돼요?
[지베]

Can I go home?

0763 내일 해도 돼요?

Is it okay to do it tomorrow?

0764 여기 앉아도 돼요?
[안자도]

Can I sit here?

0765 강아지 데려가도 돼요?

Is it okay to bring my dog?

0766 저 먼저 가도 돼요?

Can I leave first?

0767 회사 안 가도 돼요?

Is it okay not to go to work?

Can/May I + V? / Is it okay to + V?

0768 **이거 다 먹어도 돼요?**
[머거도]

Is it okay to eat this all?

0769 **뭐 하나 물어봐도 돼요?**
[무러봐도]

Can I ask you something?

0770 **한 대만 때려도 돼요?**
Can I hit you just one time?

Pattern 071.

 (으)면 안 돼요.

* Attach -으면 to a verb stem that ends in a consonant. Otherwise, attach -면.

0771 **가면 안 돼요.** You cannot go/leave.

0772 **그러면 안 돼요.** You should not do that.

0773 **포기하면 안 돼요.** You should not give up.

0774 **거짓말하면 안 돼요.**
[거:진말하면]
You should not lie.

0775 **지금 열면 안 돼요.** You should not open it now.

0776 **벌써 자면 안 돼요.** You cannot go to bed yet.

0777 **안 하면 안 돼요.** You cannot NOT do it.

0778 **쉽게 생각하면 안 돼요.**
[쉽:께] [생가카면]
You should not take it lightly.

You should not + V. /
You cannot + V.

0779 그쪽으로 가**면 안 돼요.**
[그쪼그로]

You should not go that way.

0780 경찰한테 거짓말하**면 안**
[거ː진말하면]
돼요.

You cannot lie to police officers.

0781 휴대폰은 전자레인지에 넣**으면 안 돼요.**
[휴대포는]　　　　　　　　[너으면]

You cannot put your cellphone in the
microwave.

Pattern 072.

[   ]고 싶은 게 있어요.

0782	하고 **싶은** 게 **있어요.** [시픈] [이써요]	There is something I want to do.
0783	먹고 **싶은** 게 **있어요.** [먹꼬] [시픈] [이써요]	There is something I want to eat.
0784	사고 **싶은** 게 **있어요.** [시픈] [이써요]	There is something I want to buy.
0785	말하고 **싶은** 게 **있어요.** [시픈] [이써요]	There is something I want to say.
0786	경은 씨한테 주고 **싶은** 게 [시픈] **있어요.** [이써요]	There is something I want to give to Kyeong-eun.
0787	한 가지 물어보고 **싶은** 게 [무러보고] [시픈] **있어요.** [이써요]	There is one thing I want to ask.
0788	한 가지 확인하고 **싶은** 게 [화긴하고] [시픈] **있어요.** [이써요]	There is one thing I want to check.

There is something I want to + V.

0789
거기 가면 먹고 **싶은 게**
[먹꼬] [시픈]
있어요.
[이써요]

There is something I want to eat if I go there.

0790
언젠가 해 보고 **싶은 게**
[시픈]
있어요.
[이써요]

There is something I want to try someday.

0791
거기 가면 해 보고 **싶은 게**
[시픈]
있어요.
[이써요]

There is something I want to try doing if I go there.

0792
아무한테도 말 안 하고 **싶은 게 있어요.**
[시픈] [이써요]
There is something I do not want to tell anyone.

Pattern 073.

[   ] (으)ㄹ 뻔했어요.

0793 **울 뻔했어요.**
[뻔해써요]

I almost cried.

0794 **믿을 뻔했어요.**
[미들]   [뻔해써요]

I almost believed it.

0795 **넘어질 뻔했어요.**
[너머질]   [뻔해써요]

I almost tripped.

0796 **오해할 뻔했어요.**
[뻔해써요]

I almost misunderstood.

0797 **떨어질 뻔했어요.**
[떠러질]   [뻔해써요]

I almost fell down.

0798 **잊어버릴 뻔했어요.**
[이저버릴]   [뻔해써요]

I almost forgot.

0799 **버스를 놓칠 뻔했어요.**
[버쓰/뻐쓰를][녿칠] [뻔해써요]

I almost missed the bus.

0800 **비행기를 놓칠 뻔했어요.**
[녿칠]   [뻔해써요]

I almost missed the flight.

I almost + V-ed.

0801 반지를 잃어버릴 **뻔했어요.**
[이러버릴] [뻔해써요]
I almost lost my ring.

0802 목도리를 놓고 갈 **뻔했어요.**
[목또리를] [노코] [뻔해써요]
I almost left without my scarf.

0803 휴대폰을 변기에 떨어뜨릴 **뻔했어요.**
[휴대포늘] [떠러뜨릴] [뻔해써요]
I almost dropped my phone in the toilet.

Pattern 074.

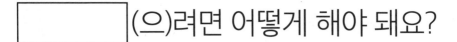

| | (으)려면 어떻게 해야 돼요?

* Attach -으려면 to a verb stem that ends in a consonant. Otherwise, attach -려면.

0804 예약하려면 어떻게 해야
[예야카려면]   [어떠케]
돼요?

What should I do in order to make a reservation?

0805 반품하려면 어떻게 해야
[어떠케]
돼요?

What should I do in order to return it?

0806 안 넘어지려면 어떻게 해야
[너머지려면]   [어떠케]
돼요?

What should I do in order not to trip?

0807 빨리 외우려면 어떻게 해야
[어떠케]
돼요?

What should I do in order to memorize it quickly?

0808 할인 받으려면 어떻게 해야
[하린] [바드려면] [어떠케]
돼요?

What should I do in order to get a discount?

0809 축구를 잘하려면 어떻게
[축꾸를]   [어떠케]
해야 돼요?

What should I do in order to be good at soccer?

0810 이거 주문하려면 어떻게
[어떠케]
해야 돼요?

What should I do in order to order this?

What should I do in order to + V?

0811 필터를 교체하**려면 어떻게 해야 돼요?**
[어떠케]

What should I do in order to change the filter?

0812 시간 관리를 잘하**려면**
[괄리를]
어떻게 해야 돼요?
[어떠케]

What should I do in order to be good at managing time?

0813 주연 씨한테 연락하**려면**
[열라카려면]
어떻게 해야 돼요?
[어떠케]

What should I do in order to contact Jooyeon?

0814 여기서 탈출하**려면 어떻게 해야 돼요?**
[어떠케]
What should I do in order to escape from here?

Pattern 075.

 (으)려면 어디로 가야 돼요?

0815 계산하려면 어디로 가야 돼요?

Where should I go in order to pay?

0816 씻으려면 어디로 가야 돼요?
[씨스려면]

Where should I go in order to wash up?

0817 지하철 타려면 어디로 가야 돼요?

Where should I go in order to take the subway?

0818 체크인 하려면 어디로 가야 돼요?

Where should I go in order to check in?

0819 짐 맡기려면 어디로 가야 돼요?
[맏끼려면]

Where should I go in order to check my baggage?

0820 시청에 가려면 어디로 가야 돼요?

Where should I go in order to get to city hall?

0821 엘리베이터 타려면 어디로 가야 돼요?

Where should I go in order to take the elevator?

0822 휴대폰 충전하려면 어디로 가야 돼요?

Where should I go in order to get my phone charged?

Where should I go in order to + V?

0823 지하 4층에 가려면 어디로
[사층에]
가야 돼요?

Where should I go in order to go to the fourth basement level?

0824 독일 가는 비행기 타려면
[도길]
어디로 가야 돼요?

Where should I go in order to take the flight to Germany?

0825 한국어 배우려면 어디로 가야 돼요?
[한:구거]
Where should I go in order to learn Korean?

Pattern 076.

혹시 ⬜ (으)세요?

* (으)세요? here is the honorific form of -아/어/여요?

0826
혹시 바쁘세요?
[혹씨]

Are you busy by any chance?

0827
혹시 지루하세요?
[혹씨]

Are you bored by any chance?

0828
혹시 어디 아프세요?
[혹씨]

Are you sick by any chance?

0829
혹시 어디 가세요?
[혹씨]

Are you going somewhere by any chance?

0830
혹시 저 아세요?
[혹씨]

Do I know you by any chance?

* "To know" is 알다 in Korean. When a verb stem ends with the consonant ㄹ, drop the ㄹ and add -세요.

0831
혹시 벌써 배부르세요?
[혹씨]

Are you full already by any chance?

0832
혹시 누구 기다리세요?
[혹씨]

Are you waiting for someone by any chance?

0833
혹시 여기 자주 오세요?
[혹씨]

Do you come here often by any chance?

Are you + Adj + by any chance? / Do you + V + by any chance?

0834 **혹시 무슨 고민 있으세요?**
[혹씨]   [이쓰세요]

Do you have any concerns by any chance?

0835 **혹시 노래방 자주 가세요?**
[혹씨]

Do you go to the singing room often by any chance?

0836 **혹시 저 싫어하세요?**
[혹씨]   [시러하세요]

By any chance, do you hate me?

Pattern 077.

언제부터 ┌ -아/어/여 ┐ 써어요?

0837 **언제부터 아팠어요?**
[아파써요]

Since when have you been sick?

0838 **언제부터 이랬어요?**
[이래써요]

Since when has it been like this?

0839 **언제부터 기다렸어요?**
[기다려써요]

Since when have you been waiting?

0840 **언제부터 팬이었어요?**
[패니어써요]

Since when have you been his/her fan?

0841 **언제부터 알고 있었어요?**
[이써써요]

Since when have you known?

0842 **언제부터 거기 있었어요?**
[이써써요]

Since when have you been there?

0843 **언제부터 여기서 일했어요?**
[일해써요]

Since when have you been working here?

0844 **언제부터 그렇게 생각했어요?**
[그러케] [생가캐써요]

Since when have you thought that way?

Since when have you + V-ed?

0845 **언제부터** 저를 **좋아했어요?**
[조아해써요]

Since when have you liked me?

0846 **언제부터** 이 일을 **했어요?**
[이:를] [해써요]

Since when have you been working in this job?

0847 **언제부터** 저를 **속였어요?**
[소겨써요]

Since when have you deceived me?

Pattern 078.

아마 ☐ (으)ㄹ 거예요.

0848 **아마 그럴 거예요.**
[그럴 꺼예요]

It is probably the case.

0849 **아마 맞을 거예요.**
[마즐 꺼예요]

It is probably right.

0850 **아마 맛있을 거예요.**
[마시쓸 꺼예요]

It is probably delicious.

0851 **아마 괜찮을 거예요.**
[괜차늘 꺼예요]

It is probably okay.

0852 **아마 꽤 비쌀 거예요.**
[비쌀 꺼예요]

It is probably quite expensive.

0853 **아마 그건 아닐 거예요.**
[아닐 꺼예요]

It is probably not the case.

0854 **아마 아직 있을 거예요.**
[이쓸 꺼예요]

It is probably still there.

0855 **아마 저한테는 작을 거예요.**
[자:글 꺼예요]

It is probably small to me.

It is probably + Adj. /
S + probably + V.

0856

그 사람은 **아마** 지금
[사:라믄]
바쁠 거예요.
[바쁠 꺼예요]

He/she is probably busy now.

0857

제 친구들이 **아마** 곧
[친구드리]
도착할 **거예요.**
[도:차칼 꺼예요]

My friends will probably arrive soon.

0858

아마 제 말이 맞을 거예요.
[마리] [마즐 꺼예요]
I am probably right.

Pattern 079.

-아/어/여 서 너무 좋아요.

* If the last syllable of a verb/adjective stem has ㅏ or ㅗ, conjugate it with -아서. Otherwise, conjugate it with -어서. Only the verb/adjective stems that end with 하 are conjugated with -여서, and 하여서 is often shortened to 해서.

** 좋아요 does not only mean "I like it" and "It is good", but it also means "I am glad."

0859	**편해서 너무 좋아요.** [조아요]	I like it so much because it is comfortable.
0860	**쉬워서 너무 좋아요.** [조아요]	I like it so much because it is easy.
0861	**잘생겨서 너무 좋아요.** [조아요]	I like him so much because he is handsome.
0862	**오늘 금요일이어서 너무** [그묘이리어서] **좋아요.** [조아요]	I am so glad that today is Friday.
0863	**경화 씨를 만나서 너무 좋아요.** [조아요]	I am so glad that I met Kyung-hwa.
0864	**시험이 끝나서 너무 좋아요.** [시허미] [끈나서] [조아요]	I am so glad that the test is over.
0865	**시간이 생겨서 너무 좋아요.** [시가니] [조아요]	I am so glad that I have some time.
0866	**날씨가 따뜻해서 너무** [따뜨태서] **좋아요.** [조아요]	I am so glad that it is warm.

I like it so much because + S + V/Adj. /
I am so glad that S + V/Adj.

0867 나무가 많아서 너무 좋아요.
　　　[마나서]　　　　　[조아요]

I am so glad that there are a lot of trees.

0868 버스　정류장이 가까워서
[버쓰/뻐쓰] [정뉴장이]
너무 좋아요.
　　[조아요]

I am so glad that the bus stop is close.

0869 저는 제가 예뻐서 너무 좋아요.
　　　　　　　　　　[조아요]

I am so glad that I am pretty.

181

Pattern 080.

제 생각에는 [＿＿＿＿＿] (으)ㄹ 것 같아요.

0870
제 생각에는 힘들 것 같아요.
[생가게는]   [힘들 껀]   [가타요]

In my opinion, it will be hard/tough.

0871
제 생각에는 괜찮을 것 같아요.
[생가게는]   [괜차늘 껀]   [가타요]

In my opinion, it will be okay/fine.

0872
제 생각에는 좋아할 것 같아요.
[생가게는]   [조아할 껀]   [가타요]

In my opinion, he/she will like it.

0873
제 생각에는 잘 어울릴 것
[생가게는]   [어울릴 껀]
같아요.
[가타요]

In my opinion, it will suit him/her well.

0874
제 생각에는 조금 작을 것
[생가게는]   [자:글 껀]
같아요.
[가타요]

In my opinion, it will be a little bit small.

0875
제 생각에는 금방 잊어버릴 것
[생가게는]   [이저버릴 껀]
같아요.
[가타요]

In my opinion, he/she will forget it soon.

0876
제 생각에는 다시 안 올 것
[생가게는]   [아 놀 껀]
같아요.
[가타요]

In my opinion, he/she will not come again.

* People will flow the pronunciation of 안 into 올 것 in this sentence.

In my opinion, S + will + V. / In my opinion, S + will be + Adj.

0877
제 생각에는 이게 더 나을 것
[생가게는]   [나을 껃]
같아요.
[가타요]

In my opinion, this one will be better.

0878
제 생각에는 이번 시험
[생가게는]
어려울 것 같아요.
[어려울 껃]   [가타요]

In my opinion, this exam will be difficult.

0879
제 생각에는 양이 너무 적을 것
[생가게는]   [저:글 껃]
같아요.
[가타요]

In my opinion, the portion will be too small.

0880
제 생각에는 제가 제일 잘할 것 **같아요.**
[생가게는]   [잘할 껃]   [가타요]
In my opinion, I will do better than everyone else.

Pattern 081.

☐ (으)ㄹ 수도 있어요.

0881
모를 수도 있어요.
[모를 쑤도]　　　[이써요]

They might not know.

0882
아닐 수도 있어요.
[아닐 쑤도]　　　[이써요]

It could be wrong.

0883
그럴 수도 있어요.
[그럴 쑤도]　　　[이써요]

It could be the case.

0884
어려울 수도 있어요.
[어려울 쑤도]　　　[이써요]

It could be difficult.

0885
어지러울 수도 있어요.
[어지러울 쑤도]　　　[이써요]

You might feel dizzy.

0886
그게 나을 수도 있어요.
　　　[나을 쑤도]　　　[이써요]

It might be better.

0887
좀 시끄러울 수도 있어요.
　　　[시끄러울 쑤도]　　　[이써요]

It could be a bit noisy.

0888
조금 아플 수도 있어요.
　　　[아플 쑤도]　　　[이써요]

It could hurt a little bit.

It could be that + S + V. /
S + might + V.

0889

생각한 거랑 다를 **수도**
[생가칸]　　　　　[다를 쑤도]
있어요.
[이써요]

It might be different from what
you thought.

0890

경은 씨 말이 맞을 **수도**
　　　　[마리]　[마즐 쑤도]
있어요.
[이써요]

What Kyeong-eun said could
be right.

0891　거짓말일 **수도 있어요.**
　　[거:진마릴 쑤도]　　　[이써요]
It could be a lie.

Pattern 082.

만약 ⬚ (으)면 어떡해요?

0892 **만약 늦으면 어떡해요?**
[마ː낙] [느즈면] [어떠캐요]

What if we are late?

0893 **만약 재미없으면 어떡해요?**
[마ː낙] [재미업쓰면] [어떠캐요]

What if it is not fun?

0894 **만약 안 되면 어떡해요?**
[마ː낙] [어떠캐요]

What if it does not work?

0895 **만약 갑자기 아프면**
[마ː낙] [갑짜기]
어떡해요?
[어떠캐요]

What if you get sick all of a sudden?

0896 **만약 거기 없으면**
[마ː낙] [업쓰면]
어떡해요?
[어떠캐요]

What if it is not there?

0897 **만약 너무 어두우면**
[마ː낙]
어떡해요?
[어떠캐요]

What if it is too dark?

0898 **만약 너무 어려우면**
[마ː낙]
어떡해요?
[어떠캐요]

What if it is too difficult?

What if + S + V/Adj?

0899
만약 화장실에 가고 싶**으면**
[마:냑] [화장시레] [시프면]
어떡해요?
[어떠캐요]

What if I want to go the restroom?

0900
만약 사람이 너무 많**으면**
[마:냑] [사:라미] [마느면]
어떡해요?
[어떠캐요]

What if there are too many people?

0901
만약 손님이 한 명도 없**으면**
[마:냑] [손니미] [업쓰면]
어떡해요?
[어떠캐요]

What if there is not even one customer?

0902
만약 이 사람이 저한테 고백하**면 어떡해요?**
[마:냑] [사:라미] [고배카면] [어떠캐요]

What if this person confesses to me?

Pattern 083.

그렇기는 하지만 │ -아/어/여│요.

0903	그렇기는 하지만 아쉬워요. [그러키는]	That is true, but it is a shame.
0904	그렇기는 하지만 [그러키는] 실망스러워요.	That is true, but it is disappointing.
0905	그렇기는 하지만 아직은 [그러키는]　　　　　[아지근] 몰라요.	That is true, but we do not know yet.
0906	그렇기는 하지만 어쩔 수 [그러키는]　　　　　[어쩔 쑤] 없어요. [업써요]	That is true, but we have no other choice.
0907	그렇기는 하지만 조용해서 [그러키는] 좋아요. [조아요]	That is true, but I like it here because it is quiet.
0908	그렇기는 하지만 멀어서 [그러키는]　　　　　[머러서] 불편해요.	That is true, but it is inconvenient because it is too far.
0909	그렇기는 하지만 많이 [그러키는]　　　　　[마니] 어렵지는 않아요. [어렵찌는]　　　[아나요]	That is true, but it is not too difficult.

That is true, but + S + V.

0910 그렇기는 하지만 시간이
[그러키는] [시가니]
별로 없어요.
[업써요]

That is true, but we are running out of time.

0911 그렇기는 하지만 이건 너무
[그러키는]
작아요.
[자:가요]

That is true, but this is too small.

0912 그렇기는 하지만 여기는
[그러키는]
사람이 너무 많아요.
[사:라미] [마나요]

That is true, but there are too many people here.

0913 그렇기는 하지만 좀 의심스러워요.
[그러키는]
That is true, but it is a bit suspicious.

Pattern 084.

가끔 ⬚⬚⬚⬚ (으)ㄹ 때도 있어요.

0914 **가끔 그럴 때도 있어요.**
[이써요]

Sometimes it happens.

0915 **가끔 피곤할 때도 있어요.**
[이써요]

Sometimes it is tiring.

0916 **가끔 어지러울 때도 있어요.**
[이써요]

Sometimes I feel dizzy.

0917 **가끔 귀찮을 때도 있어요.**
[귀차늘]　　　　[이써요]

Sometimes I feel lazy.

0918 **가끔 미안할 때도 있어요.**
[이써요]

There are times when I feel bad.

0919 **가끔 잘 안 될 때도 있어요.**
[이써요]

There are times when things do not work out.

0920 **가끔 공부하기 싫을 때도**
[시를]
있어요.
[이써요]

Sometimes I do not want to study.

0921 **가끔 무릎이 아플 때도**
[무르피]
있어요.
[이써요]

Sometimes I feel pain in my knees.

Sometimes + S + V/Adj. / There are times when + S + V/Adj.

0922
가끔 남편이 미울 **때도**
[남펴니]
있어요.
[이써요]

There are times when I hate my husband.

0923
가끔 갑자기 비가 올 **때도**
[갑짜기]
있어요.
[이써요]

Sometimes it starts to rain all of a sudden.

0924 **가끔** 이유 없이 울 **때도 있어요.**
[업씨]   [이써요]
Sometimes I cry without a reason.

Pattern 085.

너무 ⬜⬜⬜ (으/느)ㄴ 거 아니에요?

* Attach -는 to a verb stem and -(으)ㄴ to an adjective stem. Attach -은 to an adjective stem that ends in a consonant. Otherwise, attach -ㄴ.

| 0925 | **너무 빠른 거 아니에요?** | Don't you think it is too fast? |

| 0926 | **너무 작은 거 아니에요?**
[자:근] | Don't you think it is too small? |

| 0927 | **너무 늦은 거 아니에요?**
[느즌] | Don't you think it is too late? |

| 0928 | **너무 좋아하는 거**
[조아하는]
아니에요? | Don't you think you like it too much? |

| 0929 | **너무 크게 웃는 거**
[운:는]
아니에요? | Don't you think you are laughing too loudly? |

| 0930 | **너무 많이 먹는 거**
[마:니] [멍는]
아니에요? | Don't you think you are eating too much? |

| 0931 | **너무 쉽게 생각하는 거**
[쉽께] [생가카는]
아니에요? | Don't you think you are taking it too lightly? |

Don't you think it is too + Adj? / Don't you think + S + V + too much?

0932	너무 많이 사는 거 [마:니] **아니에요?**	Don't you think you are buying too much?
0933	너무 가볍게 말하는 거 [가볍께] **아니에요?**	Don't you think you are talking about it too lightly?
0934	너무 진지하게 생각하는 거 [생가카는] **아니에요?**	Don't you think you are taking it too seriously?

> 0935 **너무 예쁜 거 아니에요?**
> Don't you think it is too pretty?

193

Pattern 086.

그건 너무 ☐ .

0936	**그건 너무** 비싸요.	That is too expensive.
0937	**그건 너무** 짧아요. [짤바요]	That is too short.
0938	**그건 너무** 무거워요.	That is too heavy.
0939	**그건 너무** 어려워요.	That is too difficult.
0940	**그건 너무** 이상해요.	That is too strange.
0941	**그건 너무** 이기적인 [이:기저긴] 말이에요. [마:리에요]	That is too selfish of a statement.
0942	**그건 너무** 위험한 생각이에요. [생가기에요]	That is too dangerous of an idea.

That is too + Adj.

0943 **그건 너무** 안 어울리는
것 같아요.
[건] [가타요]

I do not think that suits you at all.

* Unless you pause between 안 and 어울리는, 안 어울리는 is pronounced as [아 너울리는].

0944 **그건 너무** 재미없는 것
[재미엄는] [건]
같아요.
[가타요]

I do not think that is fun at all.

0945 **그건 너무** 말도 안 되는
것 같아요.
[건] [가타요]

I think that is too nonsensical.

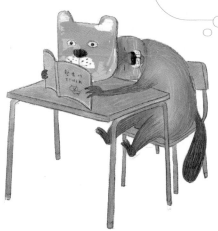

0946 **그건 너무** 유치해요.
That is too childish.

Pattern 087.

[　　　　　] 괜찮아요?

0947 이거 **괜찮아요?**
[괜차나요]

Is this okay?

0948 커피 **괜찮아요?**
[괜차나요]

Is coffee okay?

0949 거기 **괜찮아요?**
[괜차나요]

Is that place okay?

0950 오늘 시간 **괜찮아요?**
[괜차나요]

Do you have time today?

0951 매운 음식 **괜찮아요?**
[괜차나요]

Is spicy food okay?

0952 자리 바꾸는 거 **괜찮아요?**
[괜차나요]

Is it okay to switch seats?

0953 점심으로 비빔밥 **괜찮아요?**
[점:시므로]　　[비빔빱]　　[괜차나요]

Is bibimbap okay for lunch?

0954 회식 장소로 여기 **괜찮아요?**
[괜차나요]

Is this place okay for company dinner?

Is + N + okay? /
Is it okay to + V?

0955 지금 출발해도 **괜찮아요?**
[괜차나요]

Is it okay to depart now?

0956 집에 안 가도 **괜찮아요?**
[지베] [괜차나요]

Is it okay for you not to go home yet?

0957 돈 제가 다 써도 **괜찮아요?**
[괜차나요]

Is it okay for me to spend all the money?

Pattern 088.

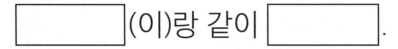

(이)랑 같이 _____.

* Attach -이랑 to a noun that ends in a consonant. Otherwise, attach -랑.

0958 동생**이랑 같이** 갈 거예요.
[가치] [갈 꺼예요]
I will go together with my younger brother/sister.

0959 친구**랑 같이** 할 거예요.
[가치] [할 꺼예요]
I will do it together with my friend.

0960 친구**랑 같이** 여행 가고
[가치]
싶어요.
[시퍼요]
I want to travel together with my friend.

0961 엄마**랑 같이** 영화 봤어요.
[가치] [봐써요]
I saw a movie with my mom.

0962 석진 씨**랑 같이** 다녀올게요.
[석찐] [가치] [다녀올께요]
I will go and come back with Seokjin.

0963 아빠**랑 같이** 산책하러
[가치] [산채카러]
갈 거예요.
[갈 꺼예요]
I will go to take a walk together with my dad.

0964 주연 씨**랑 같이**
[가치]
요리할 거예요.
[요리할 꺼예요]
I will cook together with Jooyeon.

S + V + together with + N.

0965 저랑 같이 여기에 있어
[가치]   [이써]
주세요.

Please stay here together with me.

0966 이거랑 같이 먹으면
[가치]   [머그면]
맛있어요.
[마시써요]

It tastes good if you eat these together.

0967 커피랑 같이 드셔 보세요.
[가치]

Please try it with coffee.

* 드시다 is an honorific version of 먹다.

0968 친구랑 같이 훔쳤어요.
[가치]   [훔처써요]
I stole it together with my friend.

Pattern 089.

이 중에서 뭐가 제일 [   ]?

0969
이 중에서 뭐가 제일 좋아요?
[조아요]

Which of these do you like the most? / Which of these is the best?

0970
이 중에서 뭐가 제일 예뻐요?

Which of these is the prettiest?

0971
이 중에서 뭐가 제일 나아요?

Which of these is better than the others?

0972
이 중에서 뭐가 제일 별로예요?

Which of these is the worst?

0973
이 중에서 뭐가 제일 중요해요?

Which of these is the most important?

0974
이 중에서 뭐가 제일 맛있어요?
[마시써요]

Which of these is the most delicious?

0975
이 중에서 뭐가 제일 하고 싶어요?
[시퍼요]

Which of these do you want to do the most?

* People often say "-이/가 -고 싶다" instead of "-을/를 -고 싶다" to emphasize how much they want.

Which of these is the most + Adj? / Which of these do you + V + the most?

0976	이 중에서 뭐가 제일 갖고 싶어요? [갇꼬] [시퍼요]	Which of these do you want to have the most?
0977	이 중에서 뭐가 제일 튼튼해 보여요?	Which of these looks the strongest?
0978	이 중에서 뭐가 제일 마음에 들어요? [마으메] [드러요]	Which of these do you like the most?

0979 **이 중에서 뭐가 제일** 쓸데없는 물건이에요?
[쓸떼엄는] [물거니에요]
Which of these is the most useless item?

Pattern 090.

이 중에서 하나 [   ].

0980	**이 중에서 하나** 가져가세요. [가저가세요]	Please take one out of these.
0981	**이 중에서 하나** 고르세요.	Please choose one out of these.
0982	**이 중에서 하나** 드릴게요. [드릴께요]	I will give you one out of these.
0983	**이 중에서 하나** 저 주세요.	Please give me one out of these.
0984	**이 중에서 하나** 고르면 돼요?	So I can choose one out of these?
0985	**이 중에서 하나** 골라야 돼요?	Do I have to choose one out of these?
0986	**이 중에서 하나** 주문할 수 있어요. [주문할 쑤]　　　[이써요]	You can order one out of these.
0987	**이 중에서 하나** 제가 써도 돼요?	Can I use one out of these?

S + V + one out of these.

0988 **이 중에서 하나** 기념품으로 가져가세요.
[기념푸므로]　　　[가저가세요]

Please take one out of these as a souvenir.

0989 **이 중에서 하나** 저한테 주시면 안 돼요?

Can't you give me one out of these?

0990 **이 중에서 하나** 저한테 공짜로 주세요.
Please give me one out of these for free.

Pattern 091.

이거 어떻게 [   ]?

0991 **이거 어떻게 바꿔요?**
[어떠케]
How do you change this?

0992 **이거 어떻게 먹어요?**
[어떠케] [머거요]
How do you eat this?

0993 **이거 어떻게 구했어요?**
[어떠케] [구해써요]
How did you get this?

0994 **이거 어떻게 고쳤어요?**
[어떠케] [고처써요]
How did you fix it?

0995 **이거 어떻게 만들었어요?**
[어떠케] [만드러써요]
How did you make this?

0996 **이거 어떻게 옮겼어요?**
[어떠케] [옴겨써요]
How did you move this?

0997 **이거 어떻게 입는 거예요?**
[어떠케] [임는]
How do you wear this?

* People often say "-는 거예요?" instead of "-아/어/여요?" just out of habit. However, the meanings are the same, which means you can also say "이거 어떻게 입어요?"

0998 **이거 어떻게 여는 거예요?**
[어떠케]
How do you open this?

How do you + V? /
How did you + V?

0999 **이거 어떻게 읽는 거예요?**
[어떠케] [잉는]

How do you read this?

1000 **이거 어떻게 쓰는 거예요?**
[어떠케]

How do you use this?

1001 **이거 어떻게 없애요?**
[어떠케] [업:쌔요]

How do you get rid of this?

Pattern 092.

$\boxed{}$ 기 전에 $\boxed{}$.

1002	도착하기 전에 알려 주세요. [도차카기]　[저네]	Please let me know before you arrive.
1003	후회하기 전에 그만하세요. 　　　　[저네]	Stop before you regret it please.
1004	출발하기 전에 전화해 주세요. 　　　　[저네]	Please call me before you leave.
1005	끝나기 전에 나가지 마세요. [끈나기]　[저네]	Do not leave before it is over please.
1006	해 지기 전에 돌아오세요. 　　　[저네]　[도라오세요]	Come back before sunset please.
1007	밥 먹기 전에 손 씻으세요. [밤 먹끼]　[저네]　[씨스세요]	Wash your hands before eating please.
1008	집에 가기 전에 이거 [지베]　　　[저네] 끝내세요. [끈내세요]	Finish this before you go home please.
1009	가기 전에 저하고 이야기 좀 　　[저네] 해요.	Let's have a talk before you leave.

S + V + before + V-ing.

1010 이메일 보내**기 전에** 저한테
[저네]
보여 주세요.

Please show me before you send the email.

1011 자**기 전에** 게임 해서 너무
[저네] [께임]
피곤해요.

I am so tired because I was gaming before I went to bed.

1012 화내**기 전에** 솔직히 말해요.
[저네] [솔찌키]
Before I get angry, be honest with me.

Pattern 093.

나중에 다시 [   ] .

1013	**나중에 다시** 오세요.	Come again later please.
1014	**나중에 다시** 올게요. [올께요]	I will come again later.
1015	**나중에 다시** 전화할게요. [전ː화할께요]	I will call you again later.
1016	**나중에 다시** 이야기해요.	Let's talk again later.
1017	**나중에 다시** 물어보세요. [무러보세요]	Ask me again later please.
1018	**나중에 다시** 먹어 보세요. [머거]	Eat it again later please.
1019	**나중에 다시** 확인해 [화긴해] 보세요.	Check it out again later please.
1020	**나중에 다시** 생각해 [생가캐] 보세요.	Think about it again later please.

S + V + again later.

1021 **나중에 다시** 시도해 보세요. Try it again later please.

1022 **나중에 다시** 스스로 해 보세요. Do it yourself again later please.

1023 저 지금 바쁘니까 **나중에 다시** 말해 주세요.
I am busy now, so please tell me again later.

Pattern 094.

그래도 저는 ☐.

1024 **그래도 저는** 괜찮아요.
[괜차나요]

Even so, I am okay with it.

1025 **그래도 저는** 가고 싶어요.
[시퍼요]

Even so, I want to go.

1026 **그래도 저는** 사고 싶어요.
[시퍼요]

Even so, I want to buy it.

1027 **그래도 저는** 여기
있고 싶어요.
[읻꼬] [시퍼요]

Even so, I want to stay here.

1028 **그래도 저는** 이렇게 하고
[이러케]
싶어요.
[시퍼요]

Even so, I want to do it this way.

1029 **그래도 저는** 여기에서
일하고 싶어요.
[시퍼요]

Even so, I want to work here.

1030 **그래도 저는** 이게 더 좋아요.
[조아요]

Even so, I like this more.

1031 **그래도 저는** 그냥 혼자
있을게요.
[이쓸께요]

Even so, I will stay by myself.

Even so, I + V.

1032
그래도 저는 그렇게 안 하고
[그러케]
싶어요.
[시퍼요]

Even so, I do not want to do it that way.

1033
그래도 저는 이게 더
좋은 것 같아요.
[조은] [걷]

Even so, I think this is better.

1034
그래도 저는 그 사람이 좋아요.
[사ː라미] [조아요]
Even so, I like that person.

211

Pattern 095.

제가 알기로는 ☐.

1035	**제가 알기로는** 그래요.	As far as I know, that is the case.
1036	**제가 알기로는** 여기예요.	As far as I know, it is here.
1037	**제가 알기로는** 간단해요.	As far as I know, it is simple.
1038	**제가 알기로는** 내일까지예요.	As far as I know, it is due tomorrow.
1039	**제가 알기로는** 1번이 정답이에요. [일버니] [정다비에요]	As far as I know, number one is the answer.
1040	**제가 알기로는** 경은 씨 결혼했어요. [결혼해써요]	As far as I know, Kyeong-eun is married.
1041	**제가 알기로는** 중요한 거 아니에요.	As far as I know, it is not important.
1042	**제가 알기로는** 캐시 씨 말이 맞아요. [캐씨] [마리] [마자요]	As far as I know, Cassie is right.

As far as I know, S + V.

1043 **제가 알기로는** 아직 안 끝났어요.
[끈나써요]

As far as I know, it is not over yet.

1044 **제가 알기로는** 오늘 경화 씨 생일이에요.
[생이리에요]

As far as I know, today is Kyung-hwa's birthday.

1045 **제가 알기로는** 제가 제일 예뻐요.

As far as I know, I am the prettiest.

Pattern 096.

저도 잘 모르지만 ☐.

1046
저도 잘 모르지만
괜찮을 거예요.
[괜차늘 꺼예요]

Although I do not know very well, it will be fine.

1047
저도 잘 모르지만 유명한
사람 같아요.
[가타요]

I am not sure, but I think he/she is a famous person.

1048
저도 잘 모르지만
비쌀 것 같아요.
[비쌀 껃]   [가타요]

Although I do not know very well, it seems expensive.

1049
저도 잘 모르지만 이게
맞을 것 같아요.
[마즐 껃]   [가타요]

Although I do not know very well, this one seems correct.

1050
저도 잘 모르지만 그건
안 될 것 같아요.
[될 껃]   [가타요]

Although I do not know very well, that does not seem to be possible.

1051
저도 잘 모르지만 조심하는
게 좋을 것 같아요.
[조을 껃]   [가타요]

Although I do not know very well, I think you had better be careful.

1052
저도 잘 모르지만 이미
끝난 것 같아요.
[끈난] [걷] [가타요]

I am not sure, but it seems to be over already.

I am not sure, but + S + V. / Although I do not know very well, S + V.

1053
저도 잘 모르지만 뭔가 잘못된 것 같아요.
[잘몯뙨] [걸] [가타요]

I am not sure, but there seems to be something wrong.

1054
저도 잘 모르지만 이게 처음은 아닌 것 같아요.
[처으믄]   [걸] [가타요]

Although I do not know very well, I do not think it is the first.

1055
저도 잘 모르지만 제가 막내는 아닐 것 같아요.
[망내는]   [아닐 껃]   [가타요]

I am not sure, but I do not think I am the youngest.

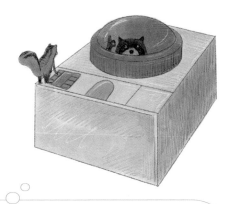

1056
저도 잘 모르지만 아무 버튼이나 눌러 볼게요.
[버트니나]   [볼께요]

I am not sure, but I will just press any button.

Pattern 097.

사실은 저 ⬚.

1057 사실은 저 올리브 싫어해요.
[사:시른] [시러해요]
In fact, I hate olives.

1058 사실은 저 그 사람 좋아해요.
[사:시른] [조아해요]
In fact, I like him/her.

1059 사실은 저 미국 사람
[사:시른]
아니에요.
In fact, I am not an American.

1060 사실은 저 영어 잘 못해요.
[사:시른] [모태요]
In fact, I cannot speak English well.

1061 사실은 저 매운 음식 못
[사:시른] [몯]
먹어요.
[머거요]
In fact, I cannot eat spicy food.

* If you say 못 먹어요 quickly, it sounds like [몬 머거요].

1062 사실은 저 미래에서 왔어요.
[사:시른] [와써요]
In fact, I am from the future.

1063 사실은 저 어제도 여기
[사:시른]
왔어요.
[와써요]
In fact, I came here yesterday too.

In fact, I + V.

사실은 저 오늘 머리 안
[사:시른]
감았어요.
[가마써요]

1064

In fact, I did not wash my hair today.

사실은 저 예지 씨한테
[사:시른]
거짓말했어요.
[거:진말해써요]

1065

In fact, I told a lie to Yeji.

사실은 저 지난주에 그
[사:시른]
영화 봤어요.
[봐써요]

1066

In fact, I watched that movie last week.

1067 **사실은 저** 천재예요.
[사:시른]
In fact, I am a genius.

Pattern 098.

이렇게 하면 ⬚ .

1068	**이렇게 하면** 돼요. [이러케]	If you do it like this, it is acceptable. / If you do it like this, it works. / You can do it like this.
1069	**이렇게 하면** 안 돼요. [이러케]	If you do it like this, it is not acceptable. / You cannot do it like this.
1070	**이렇게 하면** 끝이에요. [이러케]　　　　[끄치에요]	If you do it like this, it is done.
1071	**이렇게 하면** 더 어려워요. [이러케]	If you do it like this, it is more difficult.
1072	**이렇게 하면** 더 간편해요. [이러케]	If you do it like this, it is more convenient.
1073	**이렇게 하면** 훨씬 쉬워요. [이러케]	If you do it like this, it is way easier.
1074	**이렇게 하면** 시간이 오래 [이러케]　　　　[시가니] 걸려요.	If you do it like this, it takes a long time.

If you do it like this, S + V.

1075

이렇게 하면 현우 씨가
[이러케]   [혀누]
싫어해요.
[시러해요]

If you do it like this, Hyunwoo does not like it.

1076

이렇게 하면 캐시 씨한테
[이러케]   [캐씨]
혼나요.

If you do it like this, Cassie scolds you.

1077

이렇게 하면 사람들이
[이러케]   [사ː람드리]
욕해요.
[요캐요]

If you do it like this, people criticize you.

1078

이렇게 하면 살 안 쪄요?
[이러케]   [쪄요]
If I do it like this, I do not gain weight?

Pattern 099.

내일 시간 되면 ⬜.

1079	내일 시간 되면 산책할래요? [산채칼래요]	If you have time tomorrow, would you like to take a walk?
1080	내일 시간 되면 영화 볼래요?	If you have time tomorrow, would you like to watch a movie?
1081	내일 시간 되면 같이 [가치] 청소할래요?	If you have time tomorrow, would you like to clean with me?
1082	내일 시간 되면 운동하러 갈래요?	If you have time tomorrow, would you like to go work out?
1083	내일 시간 되면 우체국에 [우체구게] 다녀오세요.	If you have time tomorrow, please go to the post office.
1084	내일 시간 되면 은행에 갔다 오세요. [갇따]	If you have time tomorrow, please go to the bank.
1085	내일 시간 되면 저 좀 도와주세요.	If you have time tomorrow, please help me out.
1086	내일 시간 되면 저녁 같이 먹을래요? [가치] [머글래요]	If you have time tomorrow, would you like to have dinner together?

If you have time tomorrow, S + V.

1087 **내일 시간 되면** 저랑 어디 좀 갈래요?

If you have time tomorrow, would you like to go somewhere with me?

1088 **내일 시간 되면** 저랑 카페에서 공부할래요?
[까페에서]

If you have time tomorrow, would you like to study at a cafe with me?

1089 **내일 시간 되면** 목욕 좀 하세요.
[모굑]

If you have time tomorrow, please take a bath.

Pattern 100.

☐ (으)ㄹ 수도 있고,

☐ (으)ㄹ 수도 있어요.

1090 그럴 수도 있고, 아닐 수도
[그럴 쑤도]　　[일꼬]　　[아닐 쑤도]
있어요.
[이써요]

It may or may not be the case.

1091 맞을 수도 있고, 틀릴 수도
[마즐 쑤도]　　[일꼬]　　[틀릴 쑤도]
있어요.
[이써요]

It may be correct, and it may be wrong.

1092 될 수도 있고, 안 될 수도
[될 쑤도]　　[일꼬]　　[될 쑤도]
있어요.
[이써요]

It may or may not work out.

1093 이쪽일 수도 있고,
[이쪼길 쑤도]　　[일꼬]
저쪽일 수도 있어요.
[저쪼길 쑤도]　　[이써요]

It may be this way, and it may be that way.

1094 이것보다 적을 수도 있고,
[이걷뽀다]　[저:글 쑤도]　　[일꼬]
많을 수도 있어요.
[마늘 쑤도]　　[이써요]

It may be less than this, and it may be more than this.

1095 이거 때문일 수도 있고,
[때무닐 쑤도]　　[일꼬]
저거 때문일 수도 있어요.
[때무닐 쑤도]　　[이써요]

It may be because of this, and it may be because of that.

It may + V, and it may + V. / It may or may not + V.

1096

어려울 **수도 있고,** 생각보다
[어려울 쑤도]　　　[일꼬]　[생각뽀다]
쉬울 수도 있어요.
[쉬울 쑤도]　　[이써요]

It may be difficult, and it may be easier than you thought.

1097

경은 씨가 좋아할 **수도**
　　　　　　　[조아할 쑤도]
있고, 화낼 **수도 있어요.**
[읻꼬]　[화낼 쑤도]　　[이써요]

Kyeong-eun may like it, or she may be upset over it.

1098

일찍 끝날 **수도 있고,** 조금
　　　[끈날 쑤도]　　　[일꼬]
더 걸릴 수도 있어요.
　　[걸릴 쑤도]　　[이써요]

It may be over early, or it may take a little bit more.

1099

먹을 **수도 있고,** 피부에
[머글 쑤도]　　　[일꼬]
바를 수도 있어요.
[바를 쑤도]　　[이써요]

You may eat it, and you may also apply to your skin.

1100

내일은 추울 **수도 있고,** 더울 **수도 있어요.**
[내이른]　[추울 쑤도]　　　[일꼬]　[더울 쑤도]　　[이써요]
Tomorrow it may be cold, or it may be hot.

Index

Listed in Korean dictionary order

ㄱ ㄴ ㄷ ㄹ ㅁ ㅂ ㅅ ㅇ ㅈ ㅊ ㅋ ㅌ ㅍ ㅎ

거기	there	고구마	sweet potato
거리	distance	고르다	to choose, to select
거실	living room	고민	concern, problem
거짓말	lie	고민하다	to be agonizing over (something), to ponder
거짓말하다	to tell a lie		
걱정하다	to worry	고백하다	to confess
건드리다	to put one's hand onto something slightly	고양이	cat
		고장 나다	to be broken
건물	building	고장 난	broken
걷다	to walk		* This is the adjective form of 고장 나다.
걸리다	to take (time)		
걸어오다	to walk down	고치다	to fix
것	thing	곧	soon
거	thing	공룡	dinosaur
	* This is a casual and colloquial word for 것.	공부하다	to study
		공짜로	for free
게임	game	공항	airport
결혼	wedding	과목	subject
결혼기념일	wedding anniversary	관심	interest
		괜찮다	to be okay
결혼식	wedding ceremony	괴물	monster
결혼하다	to get married	교체하다	to replace
경찰	police officer	교회	church
경찰서	police station	구하다¹	to save
경호원	guard	구하다²	to find, to get, to obtain
계산하다	to calculate		
계획	plan	국내	domestic

국내 여행	domestic travel
귀신	ghost
귀찮다	to feel lazy
그	the, that
그거	it
그건	it

This word is the shorthand for 그것은.

그게	it

This word is the shorthand for 그것이.

그냥	just, without any reasons
그때	the other day

It refers to a moment in the past.

그래도	even so
그러면	then
그런	such

This word is the shorthand for 그러한.

그렇게	in that way, like that
그렇다	to be the case
그리다	to draw
그만하다	to quit, to stop
그쪽	that way
근처	near, nearby
금방	soon
금요일	Friday

급하다	to be urgent
기간	a period of time
기념품	souvenir, keepsake
기다리다	to wait
기말고사	final exam
기억하다	to remember
기자 회견	press conference
기준	standard
기차	train
길	road, street
길이	length
김밥	gimbap
김치	kimchi
까지	to (something/somewhere)
깨끗하다	to be clean
꼭	for sure, absolutely
꽃	flower
꽤	quite
꿈	dream
끝	end
끝나다	to be over
끝내다	to finish (something)
나가다	to leave, to go outside
나다	to get

나무	tree
나비	butterfly
나쁘다	to be bad
나쁜	bad * This word is the adjective form of 나쁘다.
나오다	to come out
나중에	later, later on
낙서하다	to doodle
날	day
날씨	weather
남기다	to leave (something for someone)
남자	male, man
남편	husband
낫다¹	to be cured, to be recovered
낫다²	to be better
(돈을) 내다	to pay
내려가다	to descend, to go down
내용	content
내일	tomorrow
너무	too, excessively
넓다	to be wide
넘어지다	to fall over
넣다	to put
년	counter for years

노래	song
노래방	singing room
노래하다	to sing
놀다	to hang out, to play
놀이공원	amusement park
높다	to be high
놓다	to put
놓고 가다	to put (something) and leave
놓치다	to miss (out)
누구	who
누르다	to press
눌러 보다	to trying pressing
눈	eye
뉴스	news
늦다	to be late
늦잠	oversleeping
다	all
다녀오다	to go (somewhere) and come back
다르다	to be different
다른	different * This word is the adjective form of 다르다.
다섯	five
다시	again

다운 받다	to download (something)	독일	Germany
다음	next	돈	money
다음 주	next week	돌려주다	to give (something) back
다이어트	diet	돌아가다	to go back
다치다	to be hurt	돌아오다	to come back
달	the moon	돕다	to help
답	answer	도와주다	to help
답답하다	to be frustrating/ frustrated	동네	town
		동물원	zoo
당근	carrot	동생	younger brother/ sister
당장	right now	동안	while, for
당첨되다	to win (a prize or lottery)	동영상	video
대	counter for number of times someone hits someone	되다¹	to become
		되다²	to turn out to be
		되다³	to be possible, to be okay
더	more	둘	two
덥다	to be hot	두	two
데려가다	to take (someone)		* This is used when 둘 modifies a noun or followed by a counter.
데리러 오다	to pick (someone) on		
도	too, also	둘러보다	to look around
도대체	(how/what) on earth	뒤	later, behind, back
도망가다	to run away	드라마	drama
도서관	library	드시다	to eat (honorific)
도착하다	to arrive		

들다	to hold	마시다	to drink
들어가다	to go inside	막내	the youngest
들어오다	to come inside	만	only
디자인	design	만나다	to meet
따뜻하다	to be warm	만들다	to make
따뜻한	warm	만약	if

따뜻한 — warm

* This word is the adjective form of 따뜻하다.

만약 — if

만지다 — to touch

따라가다 — to follow, to go after (someone)

많다 — to be a lot

많이 — a lot

* This word is the adverb form of 많다.

따라오다 — to follow, to come along

딸 — daughter

말다 — not to do or to quit (something)

때리다 — to hit

때문 — because, because of

말이 안 되다 — to make no sense

말하다 — to talk

떨어뜨리다 — to fall (something)

말해 주다 — to tell (someone) (something)

떨어지다 — to fall

맛 — flavor

똑똑하다 — to be smart

맛없다 — to be not tasty

뚜껑 — lid

맛있다 — to be tasty

뜨겁다 — to be hot

맞다 — to be correct, to be right

뜨거운 — hot

* This word is the adjective form of 뜨겁다.

맡기다 — to check or leave (something to the care of someone)

뜻 — meaning

매일 — every day

라면 — ramen noodles

맵다 — to be spicy

라이브 스트리밍 — live streaming

매운 — spicy

* This word is the adjective form of 맵다.

마감 — deadline

머리	head	문제	problem
먹다	to eat	묻다	to ask
먹는 거	something to eat	물	water
먹어 보다	to try eating (something)	물건	object, thing
		물어보다	to ask
먼저	first	물티슈	wet wipes
멀다	to be far	뭐	what
메뉴	a dish (on the menu)	뭔가	something, for some reason
명	counter for people		* It is used to refer to something uncertain.
명함	business card	미국	the United States
모르다	to not know	미래	future
모이다	to gather	미세 먼지	microdust
모임	gathering	미술	art
모자	hat	미술관	art gallery
목도리	scarf	미안하다	to feel bad, to feel guilty
목욕하다	to take a bath	미안해하다	to feel bad, to feel guilty
몸	body		* This phrase is used to refer to a feeling of guilt of you and also other person, whereas 미안하다 can be used only to talk about yourself.
못하다	to be bad at (something)		
무겁다	to be heavy		
무릎	knee(s)	민트	mint
무섭다	to be scary	믿다	to believe
무서운	scary	밉다	to hate (someone)
	* This word is the adjective form of 무섭다.	바꾸다	to change
무슨	what	바나나	banana

바르다	to apply to (someone/ something)
바보	idiot
바쁘다	to be busy
바지	pants
박물관	museum
반지	ring
반품하다	to return (something to the store)
받다	to receive
발	foot
밟히다	to get stepped on by
밥	rice, meal
방	room
방법	way, method
방학	vacation
배달	delivery
배부르다	to be full
배신자	betrayer
배우다	to learn
백화점	department store
버스	bus
버튼	button
번	counter for times
벌써	already
변기	toilet
별로	not particularly, not really
병원	hospital, clinic
보내다	to send
보다	to see, to look at
보디가드	bodyguard
보라색	purple
보여 주다	to show something
복권	lottery
복숭아	peach
봄	spring
불편하다	to be inconvenient, to be uncomfortable
부산	Busan
부수다	to smash
부족하다	to be short of
부터	from
분	counter for minutes
분위기	mood
분홍색	pink
불고기	bulgogi
	* A Korean dish of shredded (usually marinated) beef with vegetables
불안하다	to be anxious

비	rain	사슴	deer
비밀번호	password	사이즈	size
비빔밥	bibimbap	사진	photo, picture
	* A Korean dish of boiled rice with assorted mixtures of meats and vegetables	산	mountain
		산책하다	to take a walk
비싸다	to be expensive	살	counter for ages
비싼	expensive	살찌다	to gain weight
	* 비싼 is the adjective form of 비싸다.	삼겹살	pork belly
		상금	prize money
비웃다	to laugh at	상품	prize
비키다	to get out of one's way	새벽	dawn
비행기	airplane	생각	thought
빠르다	to be fast	생각하다	to think
빠지다	to be missed, to be lacked	생각해 보다	to try thinking
빨간색	red	생일	birthday
빨대	straw	생일 선물	birthday present
빨래하다	to do the laundry	서두르다	to be hurry
빨리	quickly, fast	서류	document
빵	bread	서비스	service
사과하다	to apologize	서울	Seoul
사다	to buy	선물	present, gift
사람	person	선생님	teacher
사랑	love	설거지	to do the dishes
사랑하다	to love	설명하다	to explain
사무실	office	세상	world
		세일	sale

싫어하다	to hate, to dislike	아침	morning
심심하다	to be bored	아파트	apartment
싸다	to be cheap	아프다	to be sick, to hurt
싸우다	to fight	안	not, no
쏟다	to spill	안 가다	not to go
쑤다	to cook (porridge)	안다	to hug
쓰다¹	to use	앉다	to sit
쓰다²	to write	알다	to know
쓰레기	trash	알리다	to notify
쓸데없다	to be useless	알아보다	to look into
씻다	to wash	앞	the front
아니다	not to be the case	앞으로	forward
아르바이트	part-time job	약	medicine
아마	maybe, probably	약속¹	promise
아무	any	약속²	plans
아무도	anyone	양	portion
아빠	dad	양말	socks
아쉽다	to be a shame, to be disappointing	얘기하다	to have a conversation with (someone)
아아	iced Americano	어둡다	to be dark

아아 의 옆
* This word is an informal shorthand for iced Americano.

아이디어	idea	어디서	where
아이스크림	ice cream	어떡하다	to do (something) in a way
아직	still, yet		

* This word is often used in the form of "어떡해요?" to mean "What should we do?"

어떤	which	여행	trip
어떻게	how	여행하기	traveling
어렵다	to be difficult	여행하다	to travel
어린아이	child	역	station
어색하다	to be awkward	연락처	contact information
어울리다	to suit (someone)	연락하다	to contact
어제	yesterday	연예인	celebrity, TV personality
어지럽다	to be dizzy		
어쩌다가	how, how on earth	열다	to open

* This word is short for 어찌하다가. It gives nuance that the speaker is surprised at how things could have ended up that way.

		영어	English
		영화	movie
		옆	next to
어쩔 수 없다	to have no other choice	예쁘다	to be pretty
언제	when	예약	reservation
언젠가	someday	오늘	today
얼굴	face	오다	to come
엄마	mom	오래	for a long time
엄청	really	오해하다	to be mistaken
없다	to not exist	올라가다	to go up
없애다	to get rid of	올라오다	to come up
엘리베이터	elevator	올리브	olive
여기	here	옮기다	to move something
여기에	here	옷	clothes
여기에서	here	와 주다	to come (for someone)
여름	summer	왕좌	throne

왕좌의 게임	*Game of Thrones*		유명하다	to be famous
왜	why		유명한	famous
외계인	alien			* This word is the adjective form of 유명하다.
외국인	foreigner		유치하다	to be childish
외우다	to memorize		은행	bank
요리하다	to cook		음식	food
욕하다	to criticize		음악	music
용돈	allowance		의견	opinion
우체국	post office		의논	discussion
운동	working out, exercise		의심스럽다	to be suspicious
운동하다	to work out, to exercise		이	this
				* This word is the adjective form of 이거.
운동화	sneakers		이거	this one
운전하다	to drive		이건	this one
울다	to cry			* This word is the shorthand for 이것은.
울리다	to make someone cry		이게	this one
웃다	to smile			* This word is the shorthand for 이것이.
월급날	payday		이기다	to win
웹사이트	website		이기적	selfish
웹사이트 주소	website address		이동하다	to move
웹툰	webcomic		이런	this kind of
위	on		이런 것	something like this
위치	position, location		이렇게	like this, this way
위험하다	to be dangerous		이렇다	to be like this

* This word is the informal shorthand for 인스타그램.

* Koreans have created this slang term, which is short for "인싸이더(insider)", that refers to those who know what is in style and get along with everyone in the group. This is basically the opposite concept of "아웃사이더 (outsider)".

* This word is the adjective form of 자세하다.

잘생기다	to be handsome
잘생긴	handsome

*This word is the adjective form of 잘생기다.

잘하다	to be good at (something)
잠깐	for a moment
잠깐만	just for a moment
잡다	to hold
장	counter for paper
장갑	gloves
장르	genre
장마	monsoon, rainy season
장미	rose
장미꽃	rose
장소	place
재미	fun
재미없다	to be not fun
저	I, me (honorific)
제	my (honorific)
저거	that thing
저기	there
저기에	there
저기서	there

*This is the shorthand for 저기에서.

저녁	evening

저녁 식사	dinner
저희	our (honorific)
저희 집	our house (honorific)
적다	to be small in amount
전	before
전부	all
전자레인지	microwave
전화하다	to make a phone call
점심	lunch
정답	answer
정류장	stop, station
정리하다	to clean, to tidy up
정말	really
정하다	to decide
정확하다	to be accurate
제	my (honorific)
제목	title
제일	the most
제주도	Jeju island

*Jeju Island is the biggest and most popular island in Korea.

조금	a little bit
좀	a little bit

*This is the shorthand for 조금.

조금만	just a little bit
조심하다	to be careful, to watch out
조용하다	to be quiet
조용한	quiet * This word is the adjective form of 조용하다.
조용히	quietly * This word is the adverb form of 조용하다.
조카	niece, nephew
졸업	graduation
졸업식	graduation ceremony
좁다	to be small in area
종	bell
종일	all day long
좋다	to be good (intransitive)
좋아하다	to like (transitive)
주다	to give
주말	weekend
주문하다	to order
주소	address
주스	juice
주유소	gas station
주차하다	to park
죽	porridge

준비	preparation
준비 운동	warm-up exercise
준비되다	to be ready
준비하다	to prepare
중간고사	midterms
중요하다	to be important
중요한	important * This is the adjective form of 중요하다.
지갑	wallet
지금	now
지난주	last week
지루하다	to be bored
지키다	to keep
지하	basement
지하철	subway
직접¹	(to do something) oneself
직접²	directly
진지하다	to be serious
진지하게	seriously * This is the adverb form of 진지하다.
질문	question
짐	baggage
집	house
짜다	to be salty
짧다	to be short

쯤	approximately, around	초등학생	elementary school student
찍다	to take (a photo/video)	초콜릿	chocolate
차¹	car	촬영하다	to film
차²	tea	추천하다	to recommend
차갑다	to be cold	축구	soccer
차가운	cold	축제	festival
	*This word is the adjective form of 차갑다.	축하하다	to celebrate, to congratulate
차례	turn	출근	going to work
착하다	to be kind, to be nice	출발하다	to depart
참다	to endure	춤	dance
찾다	to find (someone/something)	춥다	to be cold
찾아 주다	to find (something for someone)	충전하다	to charge (something)
		취미	hobby
채소	vegetables	층	floor
책	book	친구	friend
책상	desk	친구 집	friend's house
처음	first	친구들	friends
천재	genius	친하다	to be close
천천히	slowly	친한	close
청소	cleaning		*This is the adjective form of 친하다.
청소하다	to clean	카페	cafe
체크인	check-in	커피	coffee
쳐다보다	to stare	컴퓨터	computer
		컵	cup

해 보다	to try doing (something)
해외	overseas country
해외 여행	traveling abroad
핸드폰	cellphone
행사	event
행성	planet
향	scent
호랑이	tiger
호주	Australia
혹시	by any chance
혼나다	to be scolded
혼자[1]	by oneself
혼자[2]	alone
혼자서	by onesellf
화내다	to go off on (someone)
화장	make-up
화장실	restroom
확인하다	to check, to confirm
확인	confirmation

 * This is the noun form of 확인하다.

회사	company
회식	company dinner/ gathering
회원가입	signing up

회의	meeting
후추	black pepper
후회하다	to regret
훔치다	to steal
훨씬	way more
휴가	vacation, day-off
휴대폰	cellphone
힌트	hint
힘들다[1]	to be tough
힘들다[2]	to be tired

Learn More Effectively
with Our Premium Courses

Gain unlimited access to hundreds of video and
audio lessons by becoming a Premium Member on
our website, https://talktomeinkorean.com!